Extending International Human Rights Protections to Vulnerable Populations

This book inductively develops a new typology that identifies and evaluates three principal strategies that have been, and are being, used to extend international human rights protections to new categories of vulnerable populations.

The book explicates the evolution and ongoing utility of the three strategies: categorical enlargement, conceptual expansion, and group-conscious universal application. The strategies are elucidated by case studies of nine distinct vulnerable populations: national minorities; those oppressed on the basis of caste; people with albinism; cross-cultural migrants; members of the African diaspora; Roma/Gypsies; persons affected by leprosy; older individuals; and lesbian, gay, bisexual, and transgender (LGBT) people. The book concludes by considering the utility of the three strategies for emerging vulnerable populations. It encourages discourse about the protection of vulnerable populations to move beyond a stale fixation on the texts of treaties and towards a more proactive normative framework that prioritizes the lived experiences of human beings.

Extending International Human Rights Protections to Vulnerable Populations will be of key interest to students and scholars of international human rights, to social justice advocates, to human rights practitioners, and to those working with oppressed groups, human rights law, and international relations.

Raymond A. Smith is an adjunct associate professor with the Center for Global Affairs at New York University (NYU) and a faculty member of the Program in Human Rights Practice at the University of Arizona, USA.

Routledge Studies in Human Rights

Series Editors: Mark Gibney, *UNC Asheville, USA,* Thomas Gammeltoft-Hansen, *University of Copenhagen, Denmark, and* Bonny Ibhawoh, *McMaster University, Canada.*

The Routledge Human Rights series publishes high quality and cross-disciplinary scholarship on topics of key importance in human rights today. In a world where human rights are both celebrated and contested, this series is committed to create stronger links between disciplines and explore new methodological and theoretical approaches in human rights research. Aimed towards both scholars and human rights professionals, the series strives to provide both critical analysis and policy-oriented research in an accessible form. The series welcomes work on specific human rights issues as well as on cross-cutting themes and institutional perspectives.

Human Rights and US Foreign Policy
Prevarications and Evasions
Clair Apodaca

Politics of International Human Rights Law
Promotion in Western Europe
Order versus Justice
Koldo Casla

Extending International Human Rights Protections
to Vulnerable Populations
Raymond A. Smith

For a full list of titles in this series, please visit www.routledge.com

Extending International Human Rights Protections to Vulnerable Populations

Raymond A. Smith

Routledge
Taylor & Francis Group

LONDON AND NEW YORK

First published 2020 by Routledge

2 Park Square, Milton Park, Abingdon, Oxon OX14 4RN

605 Third Avenue, New York, NY 10017

Routledge is an imprint of the Taylor & Francis Group, an informa business

First issued in paperback 2021

British Library Cataloguing in Publication Data
A catalogue record for this book is available from the British Library

Library of Congress Cataloging in Publication Data
Names: Smith, Raymond A., 1967– author.
Title: Extending international human rights protections to
   vulnerable populations / Raymond A. Smith.
Description: Abingdon, Oxon ; New York, NY : Routledge, 2020. |
   Includes bibliographical references and index.
Identifiers: LCCN 2019032774 (print) | LCCN 2019032775 (ebook) |
   ISBN 9780367222093 (hardback) | ISBN 9780429273803 (ebook)
Subjects: LCSH: Human rights—Case studies. | Marginality,
   Social—Case studies. | Evaluation research (Social action
   programs)
Classification: LCC JC571 .S648 2020 (print) | LCC JC571
   (ebook) | DDC 323—dc23
LC record available at https://lccn.loc.gov/2019032774
LC ebook record available at https://lccn.loc.gov/2019032775

ISBN: 978-0-367-22209-3 (hbk)

ISBN: 978-1-03-217701-4 (pbk)

DOI: 10.4324/9780429273803

Typeset in Times New Roman
by Apex CoVantage, LLC

Contents

Acknowledgments

The author wishes to acknowledge the support of the University of Essex (UK) School of Law, and in particular its Centre for Human Rights, where this work was originally developed. I am also grateful for the encouragement and insights of a wide range of friends and associates in the United States, including those at New York University, especially at the Center for Global Affairs and the Department of Politics; the Columbia University Department of Political Science; the Division of Gender, Sexuality, and Health at the Columbia University Medical Center; and the University of Arizona College of Social and Behavioral Sciences, including the Program in Human Rights Practice and the School of Geography and Development. In addition, my thanks go to the United Nations Association of the United States (UNA-USA) and to OutRight Action International for facilitating my access to work at the United Nations, both in New York and in Geneva. The skillful guidance of the staff at Routledge is also much appreciated.

Abbreviations and acronyms

CAT	Convention against Torture and Other Cruel, Inhuman or Degrading Treatment or Punishment
CEDAW	Convention on the Elimination of All Forms of Discrimination against women
CEDAW Committee	Treaty-monitoring body of CEDAW, also called the Women's Committee
CERD	Committee on the Elimination of Racial Discrimination, treaty-monitoring body of ICERD
CESCR	Committee on Economic, Social, and Cultural Rights, treaty-monitoring body of ICESCR
CPED	International Convention for the Protection of All Persons from Enforced Disappearance
CRC	Convention on the Rights of the Child
CRPD	Convention on the Rights of Persons with Disabilities
ECOSOC	UN Economic and Social Council
GC	General Comment, issued by a treaty-monitoring body
GR	General Recommendation, issued by a treaty-monitoring body
HRC	Human Rights Council of the United Nations
HRCtte	Human Rights Committee, treaty-monitoring body for the ICCPR
ICCPR	International Covenant on Civil and Political Rights
ICERD	International Convention on the Elimination of All Forms of Discrimination
ICESCR	International Covenant on Economic, Social, and Cultural Rights
ICJ	International Court of Justice

ICMW	International Convention on the Protection of the Rights of All Migrant Workers and Members of Their Families
IE	Independent Expert, a type of UN Special Procedure
IE on Older Persons	Independent Expert on the enjoyment of all human rights by older persons
IE on PWAs	Independent Expert on the enjoyment of human rights by persons with albinism
IE on SOGI	Independent Expert on protection against violence and discrimination based on sexual orientation and gender identity
IHR	international human rights
ILC	International Law Commission of the United Nations
ILO	International Labor Organization
LGBTI	lesbian, gay, bisexual, transgender, and intersex
NGO	Non-governmental organization
OHCHR	UN Office of the High Commissioner on Human Rights
OP	Optional Protocol to a treaty
PWA	person with albinism
SOGI	sexual orientation and gender identity
SOGIESC	sexual orientation, gender identity and expression, and sex characteristics
SPs	UN Special Procedures
SR	Special Rapporteur, a type of UN Special Procedure
SR on Leprosy	Special Rapporteur on the elimination of discrimination against persons affected by leprosy and their family members
SR on Minorities	Special Rapporteur on minority issues
SR on Racism	Special Rapporteur on racism, racial discrimination, xenophobia, and related intolerance
UDHR	Universal Declaration of Human Rights
UN	United Nations
UNESCO	United Nations Educational, Social, and Cultural Organization
UNGA	United Nations General Assembly
UNICEF	United Nations Children's Fund

UPR	Universal Periodic Review of the Human Rights Council
VCLT	Vienna Convention on the Law of Treaties
VDPA	Vienna Declaration and Programme of Action
WG	Working Group, a type of UN Special Procedure
WG on AD	Working Group (WG) on persons of African descent
WHO	World Health Organization

Introduction

> Great importance must be given to the promotion and protection of
> the human rights of persons belonging to groups which have been
> rendered vulnerable . . ., the elimination of all forms of discrimina-
> tion against them, and the strengthening and more effective imple-
> mentation of existing human rights instruments.
>
> —Vienna Declaration and Programme of Action,
> Article 24 (1993)

The purpose the international human rights system established and
administered by the United Nations (UN) is manifestly to promote
and protect a range of rights enjoyed by *all* human beings. Indeed, the
opening line of the Preamble to the Universal Declaration of Human
Rights (UDHR)[1] of 1948 specifies "the recognition of the inherent
dignity and of the equal and inalienable rights of all members of the
human family." Subsequent formulations state that human rights are
enjoyed by "everyone" and "without distinction of any kind."

Nonetheless, the texts of the UDHR and its earliest successors
from the 1960s – the International Covenant on Civil and Political
Rights (ICCPR);[2] the International Covenant on Economic, Social,
and Cultural Rights (ICESCR);[3] and the International Convention on
the Elimination of All Forms of Racial Discrimination (ICERD)[4] –
also go on to enumerate limited sets of specific protected characteristics. These characteristics typically refer to type of status that are
immutable, or at least very durable; in particular, an emphasis has
been placed on race, ethnicity, sex, and religion.

A small number of subsequent treaties have placed a specific focus on other social groups and thereby brought them more clearly and comprehensively under the purview of international human rights (IHR) law. These social groups include women (the Convention on the Elimination of All Forms of Discrimination Against Women, CEDAW),[5] children (the Convention on the Rights of the Child, CRC),[6] people with disabilities (Convention on the Rights of Persons with Disabilities, CPED),[7] and migrant workers (International Convention on the Protection of the Rights of All Migrant Workers and Members of Their Families, IRMW).[8] Nevertheless, it remains empirically evident that existing enumerations of protected characteristics are not always sufficient to extend protections to numerous groups that are subject to severe and systematic violations of their human rights. However, if IHR law is to achieve its aspirations to be a system that is comprehensive and universal, it must be able to organically evolve to protect *all* people. This certainly includes members of vulnerable populations whose defining characteristics do not clearly or completely fit within an existing protected category.

Such groups, as noted in the opening quotation above from the highly influential Vienna Declaration and Programme of Action (VDPA) of 1993, require "promotion and protection" of their human rights and "the elimination of all forms of discrimination against them."[9] The VDPA also notes that these goals can be achieved, at least in part, by "the strengthening and more effective implementation of existing human rights instruments" as opposed to the creation of new instruments. This is crucial, considering that the process of conceptualizing, drafting, and bringing an international convention into force is long and laborious, and thus not usually a viable model for ensuring the timely coverage of additional categories of vulnerable populations. For example, 27 years elapsed between the UDHR (1948) and the ICERD (1965), with yet another 41 before the advent of the most recent IHR treaty, the Convention on the Rights of Persons with Disabilities[10] (CRPD, 2006).

In a few cases, Optional Protocols (OPs) have been introduced to existing treaties, such as the Second OP to the ICCPR, aiming to abolish the death penalty.[11] However, this process is nearly as difficult to achieve as a new treaty; the Second OP was adopted 24 years after the ICCPR itself and today has only half the number of States Parties as its parent treaty.[12] Even less viable, however, is the idea of adding textual amendments to existing treaties, given the near-impossibility of achieving consensus in favor of alterations to multilateral international agreements that span disparate States Parties from around the world.

Considering these constraints, this book addresses the central question: *Given the limited scope of the protected characteristics specifically enumerated within the text of IHR treaties, what strategies have been developed and deployed to successfully extend international human rights protections to new categories of vulnerable populations?* This book takes the position that a great deal can be accomplished within the existing parameters of IHR law through the "evolutive interpretation" of the law by means of so-called "soft law" processes. More specifically, this book inductively develops and explicates a new typology of three principal strategies that have been, and are being, used. These comprise the following:

- *Categorical enlargement*: the (re-)interpretation of an existing protected characteristic to include a related or adjacent category of vulnerable population that may not originally have been considered to fall under that protected characteristic.
- *Conceptual expansion*: the deployment of novel heuristic frameworks that have no fixed existing definitions under IHR law but are needed to fully ascertain and address complex patterns of intersectional and compounded discrimination that are unique to particular vulnerable populations.
- *Group-conscious universal application*: the approach that universal rights can effectively be defended either by identifying distinct social groups as falling under broad "other status" provisions or, more fundamentally, through the recognition that effective universal defense of individuals requires attention to the group-level characteristics that contribute to their vulnerability.

This book provides nine case studies in which these three strategies have been employed and considers their potential for extending human rights protections to diverse categories of vulnerable groups. Given that this book is particularly oriented towards the current and ongoing protection of emerging new categories, it places an emphasis on examples that have been initiated since about the year 2000 and are still in development.

Chapter 1 maps out the scope of existing protected characteristics under IHR "hard law," as promulgated through the UN system, which is limited to 27 enumerated characteristics and overlooks numerous other sources of vulnerability to human rights violations. Chapter 1 then turns to the doctrine of the "evolutive interpretation" of treaties, whereby the text of treaties is to be interpreted based on norms and conditions prevailing at the time that the treaty is being *applied*, and not necessarily at the time that it was originally *drafted*. Although evolutive interpretation is most commonly carried out by courts of law, this chapter will explain the relevance of UN-based IHR "soft law" processes. Key among these are declarations and resolutions by the General Assembly, the Human Rights Council, and other political bodies of the United Nations; authoritative interpretations and decisions made by UN treaty-monitoring bodies; the work of UN Special Procedures, such as Special Rapporteurs; and programs carried out by UN offices and agencies. The chapter concludes by examining the particular legal utility of the paradigm of "vulnerability" under IHR law.

Chapter 2 examines the possibilities and limitations of the strategy of *categorical enlargement*, which entails the (re-)interpretation of an existing protected characteristic to include a related or adjacent category of vulnerable population that may not originally have been considered to fall under that protected characteristic. This chapter first considers the term "minorities," a concept with great potential for the protection of vulnerable populations but that thus far undergone only very limited categorical enlargement. It then goes on to examine the more successful ways in which elements of anti-racism protections have undergone categorical enlargement to cover caste-based oppression under the characteristic of "descent" and to classify discrimination against persons with albinism under the characteristic of "colour."[13]

Chapter 3 considers the use of *conceptual expansion*, which is the deployment of novel heuristic frameworks that have no fixed existing definition under IHR law but are argued to be necessary to fully ascertain and address complex patterns of intersectional and compounded discrimination that are unique to particular vulnerable populations. Chapter 3 focuses on three prominent examples: the introduction of the concept of "xenophobia" to denote a broadly "anti-stranger" and "anti-foreigner" bias against cross-cultural migrants; the creation of the term "Afrophobia" with regard to bias against members of the

African diaspora; and the framing of a "multifaceted universe" of Roma/Gypsy peoples to better capture the complex nature of these diverse communities.

Chapter 4 reviews the strategy of *group-conscious universal application*, which represents a proactive reassertion of the starting point of all IHR law, namely its application to all individual human beings. This strategy contends that fully understanding some patterns of human rights violations requires the use of a group-specific lens – even if that group's shared characteristic is not explicitly found within the texts of IHR instruments. It argues that universal rights can effectively be defended either by identifying distinct social groups as falling under broad "other status" provisions or, more fundamentally, through the recognition that effective universal defense of individuals sometimes requires recognition of the group-level characteristics that contribute to their vulnerability. The principal case studies included in Chapter 4 are: persons affected by leprosy, as a distinct group suffering from an ancient stigma in the modern world; older persons, as a group defined by a distinctive and vulnerable position within the human life course; and lesbian, gay, bisexual, and transgender people, as a population who possess a minority sexual orientation or gender identity that renders them vulnerable to multiple forms of oppression.

The Conclusion provides a comparison of the three strategies, recognizing that they are non-mutually exclusive and can interact synergistically. It also explicates the applicability of the three strategies to emerging vulnerable populations such as those with non-binary gender expression, people susceptible to discrimination on the basis of their genetic information, and intersex persons.

Before proceeding into a consideration of the three strategies, a few brief points of clarification are in order regarding the nomenclature used in this book regarding new categories of vulnerable populations under IHR law.

The first point is that most of the groups discussed in this text are "new" only in the sense that their explicit recognition under IHR law has taken place comparatively recently and remains incomplete. In fact, many of the groups themselves, the shared characteristic(s) that define them, and the forms of human rights violations that they experience, are generally of very long standing. The recency with which their needs may have come to be addressed by the international system should be considered a shortcoming of the system of IHR law rather than of the groups themselves in any way.

A second point is that the term "group" is used here in its ordinary English-language meaning of an assemblage that is collectively identified (by its own members and/or by others) as being defined by some common characteristic. In some cases, such groups may intersect with larger debates over "group rights" – such as those that may be considered to belong to certain indigenous peoples. However, the focus in this book is solidly on the rights of the individuals *within* such groups rather than on any rights that might be said to reside within the groups themselves. This book, then, largely is largely guided by the heuristic established by Kymlicka, which refers not to "group rights" per se but rather the "group-differentiated rights" in which the rightsholders remain individuals.[14] In pursuit of neutral terminology, this book also frequently refers to "populations," a term which can be understood to refer roughly interchangeably with the ordinary meaning of the word "group" rather than any of its more specialized meanings.

A third point is that the focus of this book is exclusively at the international, or global, level. It is also specific to the corpus of international human rights law, as opposed to other related legal regimes, such as international criminal law, international humanitarian law, or international refugee law. Alongside the system of IHR law, which is focused within the UN system, there are also important regional human rights systems in Europe, Africa, and the Americas. These systems include various courts, commissions, and other organs that are called upon to define and apply various provisions from regional human rights treaties. The treaties establishing and governing the regional systems all have certain similarities to one another as well as to the IHR law system and to the universal documents. However, they also all have some significant differences, as well as distinct jurisprudences, philosophies, and processes. The activities of these systems – and, for that matter, of national-level legal systems – therefore cannot be regarded as having a direct authority with regard to the universal human rights framework. While rulings from such bodies do certainly contribute to larger currents of thought, and can have considerable persuasive value, they are beyond the scope of this book.

A final caveat is also warranted: the goal of this book is decidedly *not* to advocate for a proliferation of ever smaller and more specialized groups seeking recognition as an end in itself. Nor certainly does it seek to worsen the problem of the "hypertrophy" of human rights, or the open-ended articulation of entirely new rights. The goal, rather, is to identify and elaborate upon the many existing tools *already* available under the acquis of the IHR law regime, and to inductively develop a new typology that identifies and evaluates the three principal strategies of categorical enlargement, conceptual expansion, and group-conscious universal application.

Notes

1 UN General Assembly, *Universal Declaration of Human Rights*, 10 December 1948.
2 UN General Assembly, *International Covenant on Civil and Political Rights*, 16 December 1966.
3 UN General Assembly, *International Covenant on Economic, Social and Cultural Rights*, 16 December 1966.
4 UN General Assembly, *International Convention on the Elimination of All Forms of Racial Discrimination*, 21 December 1965.
5 UN General Assembly, *Convention on the Elimination of All Forms of Discrimination against Women*, 18 December 1979.
6 UN General Assembly, *Convention on the Rights of the Child*, 20 November 1989.
7 UN General Assembly, *Convention on the Rights of Persons with Disabilities*, 13 December 2006.
8 UN General Assembly, *International Convention on the Protection of the Rights of All Migrant Workers and Members of Their Families*, 18 December 1990.
9 UN General Assembly, *Vienna Declaration and Programme of Action*, 12 July 1993.
10 UN General Assembly, *Convention on the Rights of Persons with Disabilities*, 13 December 2006.
11 UN General Assembly, *Second Optional Protocol to the International Covenant on Civil and Political Rights, Aiming at the Abolition of the Death Penalty*, 15 December 1989.
12 UN Office of the High Commissioner for Human Rights, "Status of Ratification," accessed at https://en.wikipedia.org/wiki/Office_of_the_United_Nations_High_Commissioner_for_Human_Rights on 19 May 2019.
13 The US spelling of the "color" will generally be used below, except in direct quotations in which the original spelling was "colour." The same practice will be applied to other comparable spelling discrepancies.
14 Kymlicka, Will, *Multicultural Citizenship: A Liberal Theory of Minority Rights*, Clarendon: Oxford, UK 1995.

1 The scope of existing protections

Protected characteristics in the core international human rights treaties

Virtually every part of the enterprise of human rights is attuned to the protection of people who face conditions of particular vulnerability. However, in the texts of the major UN human rights instruments, the number of explicitly protected characteristics is quite limited. Table 1.1 provides a summary and overview of the characteristics specified in the texts of the nine core UN human rights treaties.

There is a tension inherent in the universality of these human rights conventions and their overall focus on individual rights alongside their inclusion of enumerated lists of group-level characteristics. As noted by Heinze,

> The Universal Declaration enunciates yet distrusts categories. Its abstract individualism suggests that it, ideally, would by-pass altogether this construction of difference. In practice, however, it cannot do so. It is compelled to acknowledge that differences are in fact drawn. Yet it declines to construe those categories as grounds for recognizing different kinds of rights for different kinds of persons.[1]

As tabulated in Table 1.2, there are 27 such different characteristics, including variant phrasings or formulations of characteristics and the open-ended term "other status," found in the text of these human rights instruments. Most commonly, these are found in the context of non-discrimination provisions, and typically they refer to

Table 1.1 Protected characteristics in the texts of the core IHR treaties

International treaty	*Protected characteristics (earliest usage or formulation of a term is noted in bold)*
International Convention on the Elimination of All Forms of Racial Discrimination (ICERD), 1965, Article 1(1)	"**race, colour, descent, or national or ethnic origin**"
International Covenant on Economic, Social and Cultural Rights (ICESCR), 1966, Article 2(2)	"distinction of any kind, such as race, colour, **sex, language,** religion, political or other opinion, national or **social origin, property, birth** or **other status**"
International Covenant on Civil and Political Rights (ICCPR), 1966, Article 2(1)	"distinction of any kind, such as race, colour, sex, language, religion, political or other opinion, national or social origin, property, birth or other status"
International Covenant on Civil and Political Rights (ICCPR), 1966, Article 27	"**ethnic, religious or linguistic minorities**"
Convention on the Elimination of All Forms of Discrimination against Women (CEDAW), 1979, Article 1	"sex" "**marital status**"
Convention against Torture and Other Cruel, Inhuman or Degrading Treatment or Punishment (CAT), 1984	*No grounds of non-discrimination specified*
Convention on the Rights of the Child (CRC), 1989, Article 2(1)	"the child's or his or her **parent's or legal guardian's** race, colour, sex, language, religion, political or other opinion, national, ethnic or social origin, property, **disability**, birth or other status"
International Convention on the Protection of the Rights of All Migrant Workers and Members of Their Families (ICMW), 1990, Article 1(1)	"sex, race, colour, language, religion or **conviction**, political or other opinion, national, ethnic or social origin, **nationality, age, economic position**, property, marital status, birth or other status"

(Continued)

Table 1.1 (Continued)

International treaty	Protected characteristics (earliest usage or formulation of a term is noted in bold)
International Convention for the Protection of All Persons from Enforced Disappearance (CPED), 2006, Article 13(7)	"sex, race, religion, nationality, ethnic origin, political opinions or **membership of a particular social group**," specifically as a ground for discrimination in extradition proceedings
Convention on the Rights of Persons with Disabilities (CRPD), 2006, Preamble (p)	"race, colour, sex, language, religion, political or other opinion, national, ethnic, **indigenous** or social origin, property, birth, age or other status," disability

Table 1.2 Frequency of inclusion of protected characteristics in the texts of the core IHR treaties

Protected characteristic (and number of mentions) by thematic clusters

"race" (7)
"racial group" (1)
"colour" (6)

"religion" (6)
"conviction" (1)
"religious minorities" (1)

"sex" (7)
"marital status" (2)

"other status" (5)
"membership of a particular social group" (1)

"ethnic origin" (5)
"ethnic minorities" (1)
"indigenous origin" (1)

"language" (5)
"linguistic minorities" (1)

"national origin" (5)
"nationality" (1)

"birth" (5)
"descent" (1)
"parent or legal guardian" (1)

"political opinion" (5)
"other opinion" (4)
"social origin" (5)
"property" (5)
"economic position" (1)

"age" (2)

"disability" (2)

characteristics that are durable, if not immutable. The characteristics are frequently ascriptive at the time of birth, although some may be achieved in later life (e.g., through religious conversion).

Most of the characteristics are presented as "subordinate" norms that "prohibit discrimination only in the enjoyment of rights and freedoms set forth in the respective instrument."[2] For example, the Convention on the Rights of the Child (CRC) Article 2(1) specifies that

> States Parties shall respect and ensure the rights set forth in the present Convention to each child within their jurisdiction without discrimination of any kind, irrespective of the child's or his or her parent's or legal guardian's race, colour, sex, language, religion, political or other opinion, national, ethnic or social origin, property, disability, birth or other status.[3]

In such cases, the rights ensured apply only to the enumerated list of protected characteristics and only with regard to the rights specifically covered within the treaty itself.

However, another important type of non-discrimination provision establishes "autonomous" norms that "guarantee non-discrimination not only in the context of other rights but in general."[4] The clearest of these is International Covenant on Civil and Political Rights (ICCPR) Article 26, which states "all persons are equal before the law and are entitled to equal protection of the law." In the landmark case of *Broeks v. Netherlands* from 1987, the Human Rights Committee established that this applies to all elements of the law, not simply to those pertaining to a specific civil or political right identified within the ICCPR.[5] Article 26 has at times formed the basis for recognition of the vulnerability of certain groups by the Human Rights Committee, notwithstanding that the text of Article 26 itself enumerates no specific characteristics.

It should also be noted that some references to vulnerable groups or populations are made in contexts other than the prohibition of discrimination. For example, ICCPR Article 27 emphasizes state non-interference in its requirement that ethnic, religious, and linguistic "minorities shall not be denied the right, in community with the other members of their group, to enjoy their own culture."

Further, some of the core treaties also specify special, relatively narrow protections to be afforded to certain groups. For example,

ICCPR Article 6(5) prohibits the application of the death penalty to those below the age of 18 and to pregnant women, while International Covenant on Economic, Social and Cultural Rights (ICESCR) Article 7a(i) specifies equal remuneration in employment for women and Article 10(1) requires that special assistance measures be taken on behalf of children. Such provisions are not reflected in Tables 1.1 and 1.2, as they are situation-specific rather than of universal application, but they may nonetheless offer important human rights protections under certain circumstances.

Soft law processes and the evolutive interpretation of protected characteristics

Since the various protected characteristics are not directly defined in the texts themselves, much of the work of specifying their content and substance is left to subsequent processes. The most important source with regard to the interpretation of the meaning of treaties, once they are in force, is the Vienna Convention on the Law of Treaties (VCLT).[6] The VCLT was adopted only in 1969, and thus *after* the enactment of several major human rights treaties. And as with all treaties, its direct application is limited to its States Parties. However, the VCLT was designed by the International Law Commission of the United Nations specifically to codify existing practices within customary international law, which is regarded as binding on all states unless they have demonstrated a persistent objection. Therefore, the VCLT and its provisions are widely considered to apply to all treaties and to all states.[7]

In Article 31(1), the VCLT states: "A treaty shall be interpreted in good faith in accordance with the ordinary meaning to be given to the terms of the treaty in their context and in the light of its object and purpose." "Context" is then defined to include the text, preamble, and annexes, as well as other related agreements and instruments accepted by all parties. This may later be supplemented by any subsequent agreements or practices that arise during the application of the treaty that establish "the agreement of the parties regarding its interpretation." Should such evidence still be insufficient, Article 32 allows that "[r]ecourse may be had to supplementary means of interpretation, including the preparatory work of the treaty and the circumstances of its conclusion."

The VCLT thus aims to balance "good faith" and "ordinary meaning" with "context" and "object and purpose." The latter two factors both provide crucial insight into the intentions of the enacting States Parties. Often, however, there is a tension between "contemporaneous" interpretation, in which terms are defined at the time the treaty was *written*, and an "evolutive" (also called "evolutionary" or "dynamic") interpretation, in which terms are defined at the time that a treaty is *applied*. In 2009 the International Court of Justice (ICJ) definitively took the side of evolutive interpretation when it ruled in *Dispute regarding Navigational and Related Rights*.[8] In this ruling, the ICJ specified that that an 1858 treaty to regulate commerce between Nicaragua and Costa Rica must be interpreted to comprise forms of contemporary commerce – including mechanized modes of transportation that did not exist technologically in 1858 – since to do otherwise would thwart the object and purpose of the treaty.[9]

In the context of international human rights (IHR) treaties, it is particularly well-established

> that a dynamic or 'living instrument' approach applies, according to which a human rights treaty guarantee is to be interpreted in accordance with the standards prevalent in the parties to the treaty at the time the treaty is interpreted, not those accepted by them when the treaty was adopted.[10]

In such cases, the "object and purpose" test is of particular salience. This is because IHR treaties are not of a contractual nature, unlike most treaties, through which states seek to derive benefits for themselves through their interactions with other states. Rather, IHR treaties seek principally to influence how states will treat their *own* populations, while also cultivating international norms that are broadly protective of human dignity. For example, the shared Preamble of the ICCPR and the ICESCR identifies as key goals of the instruments the "recognition of the inherent dignity and of the equal and inalienable rights of all members of the human family" (para 2); "the ideal of free human beings enjoying freedom from fear and want" (para 4); and the promotion of "universal respect for, and observance of, human rights and freedoms" (para 5).

Such broad goals demand a flexible and dynamic approach to treaty interpretation, a reality that has been confirmed by several treaty-monitoring bodies. For example, the Human Rights Committee has stated that the ICCPR "should be interpreted as a living instrument and the rights protected under it should be applied in the context and in the light of present-day conditions."[11] The Committee on the Elimination of Racial Discrimination (CERD) has likewise stated that it regards the International Convention on the Elimination of All Forms of Racial Discrimination (ICERD) "as a living instrument [that] must be interpreted and applied taking into [account] the circumstances of contemporary society."[12] As can then be clearly inferred, when the object and purpose of a treaty are manifestly to prevent discrimination, deter oppression, and alleviate cruelty directed at human beings, a more expansive interpretation of terms may not only be well justified but even required.

In many branches of international law, the evolutive interpretation of treaties is carried out primarily by courts and other judicial tribunals, especially the ICJ. However, human rights issues only occasionally arise in the ICJ's adjudication of disputes between states or in its release of advisory opinions. When the ICJ does address human rights issues, such as its advisory opinion regarding the wall built by Israel to separate itself from the Palestinian West Bank,[13] its decisions carry great legal weight. Nevertheless, cases such as this occur too infrequently for the ICJ to have developed a comprehensive jurisprudence concerning human rights. However, there is no alternative universal court of human rights with the ability to rule upon the meaning of the entire corpus of IHR texts. (Courts established within the regional human rights systems of Europe, the Americas, and Africa do play such a role in relation to the treaties governing those areas; however, these rulings do not have direct applicability to the interpretation of the international human rights system.)

In the absence of a universal judicial system, resort must be had to the VCLT's provision allowing for ongoing "practice" to further assist in the interpretation of the meaning of terms used in treaties. The scope of such "practice" is undefined, but in the context of multilateral treaties enacted and monitored under the auspices of the UN, it is appropriate to include a broad range of statements and activities undertaken by various UN entities as evidence of practice. Indeed, as Bjorge has argued,

> The intention of the founders of the UN Charter at San Francisco was to create a living institution, equipped with dynamic

political, administrative, and juridical organs which were intended to be competent to interpret their own powers under a flexible constituent instrument in response to new challenges.[14]

Such practice within the UN human rights system fits squarely under the rubric of "soft law," which is an insufficiently defined but increasingly important element of international law. As argued by Gammeltoft-Hansen et al., soft law is

> an increasing part of the normative standards generated through world politics and other international practice [which] has taken the form of non-binding agreements and other instruments short of positive international law. This new realm of 'soft law' can be seen to shape and impact upon the content of international law in multiple ways: from being a first step in a norm-making process, to providing detailed rules and more technical standards required for the interpretation and the implementation of existing rules of positive law.[15]

These authors continue:

> [t]his is especially the case in the area of human rights. While relatively few human rights treaties have been adopted at the UN level in the last two decades, the number of declarations, resolutions, conclusions, and principles has grown almost exponentially.

They note also that

> [i]n some areas, soft law has come to fill a void in the absence of treaty law, exerting a degree of normative force notwithstanding its non-binding character. In others areas, soft law seems to have become the battleground for interpretative struggles to both expand and delimit human rights protection in the context of existing regimes.[16]

An example of the organic development of soft law over time, in terms of both depth and complexity, can be found in the work of the Human Rights Committee with regard to the rights of women. Its first brief statement on this issue, in General Comment 4[17] in 1981, consisted of just 5 paragraphs, mostly focused on procedural matters.

By contrast in 2000, its General Comment 28[18] consisted of 33 para-graphs, delving into the disparate ways that "inequality in the enjoy-ment of rights by women throughout the world is deeply embedded in tradition, history and culture, including religious attitudes" (para 5). The shift from General Comment 4 to 28 reflected a very significant degree of evolutive interpretation of the exact same treaty text.

Within the UN system, four major processes for monitoring, interpreting, and at times de facto expanding the textual provi-sions of IHR law exist within the UN system itself. These four pro-cesses, which will provide the substance for much of this book, are in (roughly in descending order of influence on IHR law): politi-cal bodies, treaty-monitoring bodies, Special Procedures, and UN agencies and programs.

Political bodies

Political bodies are those composed of representatives of states; fore-most among these, for purposes of human rights, are the UN General Assembly, and some of its major subsidiary bodies, including its six Main Committees, the Human Rights Council, and the International Law Commission. Other political bodies significant for human rights include the Economic and Social Council (ECOSOC), the Commis-sion on the Status of Women, and, at times, the Security Council. Short of a full international treaty, "declarations" by political bodies constitute one of the most authoritative statements concerning the values to be enshrined in and respected under the regime of interna-tional human rights. Declarations made by the UN General Assem-bly often enunciate sweeping principles comparable to those laid out in treaties, usually require many years to be developed, and are ultimately enacted through consensus-building processes similar to those used for treaty-making.

Indeed, declarations have often been precursors to full treaties. For instance, the Convention on the Elimination of All Forms of Discrim-ination against Women (CEDAW), enacted in 1979, was preceded by the 1967 Declaration on the Elimination of Discrimination against Women.[19] Other declarations effectively function as supplements to treaties; for example, CEDAW was supplemented by the 1993 Dec-laration on the Elimination of Violence against Women.[20] Yet other declarations may not have (at least, so far) been succeeded by a full treaty but remain the most definitive statement available on a particular topic, such as the 2007 Declaration on the Rights of Indigenous Peoples.[21] Some remain under development and can be influential even in draft form, such as the as-yet-unenacted Declaration on the Rights of Peasants and Other People Working in Rural Areas.[22]

Declarations are proclaimed through the mechanism of a resolution, which is the key means by which political bodies can address an array of issues. While resolutions falling short of a full declaration may carry less weight in "soft law," they also are indicative of changing norms and perceptions. To take but one of countless examples, Resolution 65/215 by the General Assembly offered support for the a set of "Principles and Guidelines for the elimination of discrimination against persons affected by leprosy and their family members," which was originally developed by the Human Rights Council, and discussed further in one of the following case studies.[23]

The legal force of a declaration, or of other resolutions, clearly falls below that of a full treaty. However, such resolutions, particularly from the UN General Assembly, still carry considerable normative weight. Indeed, some legal theorists regard them as reflecting contemporary *opinio juris* among states and thus constituting customary international law.[24]

Treaty-monitoring bodies

Unlike the political bodies, treaty-monitoring bodies are led by civil society experts; there are nine principal treaty-monitoring bodies, each associated with one of the nine core IHR treaties outlined in Table 1.1. (A tenth treaty-monitoring body is associated with one of the Optional Protocols of the Convention against Torture.) The work of these bodies provides official interpretations of individual treaties by two main means: General Comments (sometimes called General Recommendations) about the meaning of treaty provisions, and Concluding Observations made in response to reports from countries that are parties to that specific treaty. In some cases, treaty-monitoring bodies are also empowered to make quasi-judicial decisions in response to individuals who allege that their human rights have been violated in contravention of a specific treaty.

While the interpretations and decisions of treaty bodies are not legally binding per se, they are the single most influential sources for the evolutive interpretation of their respective treaties. In particular with regard to General Comments and General Recommendations,

> there is an expectation that the conduct of States parties to UN human rights treaties is in line with them due to the authoritative status of the treaty bodies as watchdogs of the implementation of human rights codified under the auspices of the UN.[25]

One of the first established, and perhaps still most highly regarded, of the treaty-monitoring bodies is the (over-broadly named) Human Rights Committee, which oversees the ICCPR. An example of its evolutive interpretation with regard to women's rights was provided previously, and further examples of its work will be discussed below. Other bodies of particular relevance to vulnerable populations are those that monitor the universal economic, social, and cultural rights enshrined in the ICESCR, as well as the particular groups that are the focus of ICERD (ethnic/racial groups), CEDAW (women and girls), CRC (children), the International Convention on the Protection of the Rights of All Migrant Workers and Members of Their Families (ICMW, migrant workers), and the Convention on the Rights of Persons with Disabilities (CPED, persons with disabilities).

Depending upon circumstances, significant developments in IHR soft law can take place through any of the mechanisms of the treaty-monitoring bodies. For example, as discussed in the following case studies, it was an individual communication with the Human Rights Committee, in the *Toonen* case, that first established protections on the basis of sexual orientation[26] and Concluding Observations to a country report from India to CERD that initiated greater scrutiny of oppression on the basis of caste.[27]

Special procedures

A unique role in the process of extending protections to new categories of vulnerable groups is played by "UN Special Procedures" (SPs). As the name suggests, SPs were not originally created as a coherent set of institutional arrangements. Rather, the system of SPs, a term inclusive of Special Rapporteurs, Independent Experts, and Working Groups, has grown up *ad hoc* through individual mandates from the UN's political bodies to monitor and report on human rights either within a specific country or with regard to a particular theme. As such, SPs serve as the main entry point into the broader UN system for victims and human rights defenders from every corner of the world, offering practical forums for the promotion and protection of human rights. By most accounts, they have played a critical role in shaping the content of international human rights norms.[28]

Although the mandates of SPs require majority approval of the states casting a vote in the Human Rights Council, they have some advantages of scope and flexibility over other mechanisms for "pushing the envelope" on human rights issues. Mandate holders are neither UN staff members nor representatives of governments, but rather civil society–based experts serving for a fixed term without salary. Members of treaty-monitoring bodies are also experts, but they are constrained by the provisions of their respective treaties, whereas the SPs are able to apply a wider range of sources.

As of May 2019, the website for the Office of the High Commissioner for Human Rights (OHCHR) listed that there are 56 mandates, of which 44 are categorized as thematic and 12 as country-specific. The work of nearly all of the SPs intersects, at some points, with various vulnerable populations. However, as seen in Box 1.1, of the 44 thematic mandates, more than one-third (16) relate directly to a specific vulnerable population. Notably, 5 of the thematic mandates relating to vulnerable populations were created just since 2013, suggesting a high degree of recent dynamism in the work of SPs with regard to vulnerable populations.

Box 1.1   UN Special Procedures with thematic mandates directly relating to a specific vulnerable population

Titles of thematic UN Special Procedures active as of May 2019 (and the year it first received a mandate from the UN Human Rights Council)

Working Group of Experts on People of African Descent (2002)
Independent Expert on the enjoyment of human rights by persons with albinism (2015)

Special Rapporteur on the rights of persons with disabilities (2014)

Special Rapporteur on the situation of human rights defenders (2000)

Special Rapporteur on the rights of indigenous peoples (2001)

Special Rapporteur on the human rights of internally displaced persons (2004)

Special Rapporteur on the elimination of discrimination against persons affected by leprosy and their family members (1999)

Special Rapporteur on the human rights of migrants (1999)

Special Rapporteur on minority issues (2005)

Independent Expert on the enjoyment of all human rights by older persons (2013)

Special Rapporteur on contemporary forms of racism, racial discrimination, xenophobia and related intolerance (1993)

Special Rapporteur on the sale of children, child prostitution and child pornography (1990)

Independent Expert on protection against violence and discrimination based on sexual orientation and gender identity (2016)

Special Rapporteur on trafficking in persons, especially women and children (2004)

Special Rapporteur on violence against women, its causes and consequences (1999)

Working Group on the issue of discrimination against women in law and in practice (2010)

Source: Office of the High Commissioner of Human Rights, "Special Procedures of the Human Rights Council," accessed on May 19, 2019 at: www.ohchr.org/EN/HRBodies/SP/Pages/Welcomepage.aspx

The work of UN Special Rapporteurs, Independent Experts, and Working Groups, especially those focused on thematic mandates, are particularly well-placed to focus on emerging issues. Their formal reports, as well as responses to individual communications, can provide rich analyses of the human rights violations of vulnerable groups. Importantly, Special Procedures have the flexibility to draw upon multiple sources of IHR law in innovative ways; for this reason, their activities are especially prominent in the case studies discussed in subsequent chapters of this book.

UN offices and agencies

UN offices and agencies operate campaigns, programs, funds, institutes, and other mechanisms focused on a vast array of issues; among these, human rights figures prominently. Human rights issues are also regularly addressed in the work of numerous other entities such as UNICEF, UNESCO, and UN Women, and also by specialized agencies such as the International Labor Organization and the World Health Organization, which are largely autonomous in their operation but work in coordination with other UN entities.

With specific regard to IHR law, most activity is concentrated within the Secretariat, one of the UN's principal organs. Central to this work within the Secretariat is the OHCHR, which has as its mission statement: "to work for the protection of all human rights for all people; to help empower people to realize their rights; and to assist those responsible for upholding such rights in ensuring that they are implemented." Among its goals is to "focus attention on those who are at risk and vulnerable on multiple fronts."[29]

Unconstrained by the texts of specific treaties, by a particular mandate under Special Procedures, or by the actions of the political bodies, OHCHR is able to be particularly forward-looking and expansive in its operations – representing a "cutting-edge" of human rights within the UN system. A notable example of its operations is OHCHR's "Free and Equal" Campaign, which is discussed in one of this book's case studies. Free and Equal is

an unprecedented global UN public information campaign aimed at promoting equal rights and fair treatment of [lesbian, gay, bisexual, transgender, and intersex] LGBTI people. In 2017, UN Free & Equal reached 2.4 billion social media feeds around the world and generated a stream of widely shared materials – including powerful videos, impactful graphics and plain-language fact sheets.[30]

As such, the campaign is able to transcend the lack of consensus on LGBTI issues within UN political bodies while still remaining in line with global mainstream human rights thinking about LGBTI issues. Although the work of OHCHR does not in itself have a direct effect on the interpretation of IHR law, its strategic position provides it with considerable agenda-setting influence, as well as an ability to highlight neglected issues or to introduce new framings of existing issues.

Collectively, the human rights practice carried out by these four UN processes – political bodies, treaty-monitoring bodies, Special Procedures, and offices and agencies – contributes greatly to the articulation of the soft law component of IHR law. A useful and increasingly common framing used within these processes, and the one also adopted in this book, is the concept of "vulnerability."

The terms "vulnerable" or "vulnerability" appear only sparingly in the English-language texts of the core international human rights treaties and their optional protocols. The ICMW makes one mention in a preambular paragraph; a few other references are in Optional Protocols to the CRC. None of these specifically define the term, nor does the influential Vienna Declaration and Programme of Action of 1993 (quoted at the start of the Introduction) in its reference to "groups that have been rendered vulnerable."

In the most comprehensive study of the subject to date, Nifosi-Sutton recounts numerous uses of the vulnerability framing throughout the work of UN human rights bodies. She notes that the terms "vulnerable" and "vulnerability" can refer to the basic circumstances of all persons and our inherent human weaknesses,

> indicating a condition where by an individual is affected or can potentially be affected by physical or emotional harm. . . . Defined as such, vulnerability is universal in the sense that it unavoidably features in everyone's life or may occur in everyone's life.[31]

However, Nifosi-Sutton continues, the use of the terms "vulnerable" and "vulnerability" in a human rights setting more commonly "loses its universal scope and becomes especially relevant to the situation of specific groups of persons. These groups are regarded as being particularly exposed to harm or at higher risk of experiencing harm for various reasons and are labeled, as a result, as *vulnerable groups*."[32] In the context of human rights, she asserts that vulnerability is a very complex human condition affecting specific groups of persons whereby these persons are exposed, or potentially susceptible, to serious violations of human rights, or practices amounting to egregious violation of rights, to a greater extent than other member of society as a result of certain factors and circumstances or various combinations of them.[33]

Applying this lens of vulnerability, this book will now commence with its inductive examination of how three distinct strategies of evolutive interpretation have emerged within the IHR law system over roughly the past two decades: *categorical enlargement, conceptual expansion*, and *group-conscious universal application*. In doing so, it will provide nine brief case studies of vulnerable populations which, although excluded from the text of the core IHR treaties, have increasingly found protection under the aegis of IHR law through the cumulative effect of UN human rights processes and practices.

Notes

1 Heinze, Eric, "The Construction and Contingency of the Minority Concept," in Deirdre Fottrell and Bill Bowring, Eds., *Minority and Group Rights in the New Millenium*, Martinus Nijoff: Leiden, Netherlands 1999, p. 35.
2 Moeckli, Daniel, "Equality and Non-Discrimination," in Daniel Moeckli, Sangeeta Shah and Sandesh Sivakumaran, Eds., *International Human Rights Law*, 2nd Edition, Oxford University Press: Oxford, UK 2013, p. 161.
3 UN General Assembly, *Convention on the Rights of the Child*, 20 November 1989.
4 Moeckli, op. cit. 2, p. 162.
5 UN Human Rights Committee, *S. W. M. Broeks v. The Netherlands*, Communication No. 172/1984, 9 June 1987.
6 UN General Assembly, *Vienna Convention on the Law of Treaties between States and International Organizations or between International Organizations*, 12 March 1986.
7 Fitzmaurice, Malgosia, "The Practical Working of the Law of Treaties," in Malcolm Evans, Ed., *International Law*, 4th Edition, Oxford University Press: Oxford, UK 2010, pp. 169–170.
8 International Court of Justice, *Dispute regarding Navigational and Related Rights (Costa Rica v. Nicaragua)*, Judgment, 13 July 2009.
9 Bjorge, Eirik, *The Evolutionary Interpretation of Treaties*, Oxford University Press: Oxford, UK 2014, pp. 1–2.

10 Harris, David and Sandesh Sivakumaran, *Cases and Materials on International Law*, 8th Edition, Sweet & Maxwell: London, UK 2015, p. 680.

11 UN Human Rights Committee, *Roger Judge v. Canada*, Communication No. 829/1998, 13 August 2003.

12 UN Committee on the Elimination of Racial Discrimination, *Stephen Hagan v. Australia*, Communication No. 26/2002, 20 March 2003.

13 International Court of Justice, *Legal Consequences of the Construction of a Wall in the Occupied Palestinian Territory*, Advisory Opinion, 9 July 2004.

14 Bjorge, op. cit. 9, pp. 189–190.

15 Gammeltoft-Hansen, Thomas, Stéphanie Lagoutte and John Cerone, "Tracing the Roles of Soft Law in Human Rights," in Stéphanie Lagoutte, Thomas Gammeltoft-Hansen and John Cerone, Eds., *Tracing the Roles of Soft Law in Human Rights*, Oxford University Press: Oxford, UK, 2016, p. 1.

16 Ibid.

17 UN Human Rights Committee (HRC), *CCPR General Comment No. 4: Article 3 (Equal Right of Men and Women to the Enjoyment of All Civil and Political Rights)*, 30 July 1981.

18 UN Human Rights Committee, *CCPR General Comment No. 28: Article 3 (The Equality of Rights Between Men and Women*, 29 March 2000.

19 UN General Assembly, *Declaration on the Elimination of Discrimination against Women*, 7 November 1967.

20 UN General Assembly, *Declaration on the Elimination of Violence against Women*, 20 December 1993.

21 UN General Assembly, *Declaration on the Rights of Indigenous Peoples*, 7 September 2007.

22 Focus on the Global South, "From Dream to Reality: UN Declaration on Rights of Peasants and Other People Working in Rural Areas," accessed at https://focusweb.org/from-dream-to-reality-un-declaration-on-rights-of-peasants-and-other-people-working-in-rural-areas/ on 8 May 2019.

23 UN General Assembly, *Elimination of Discrimination against Persons Affected by Leprosy and Their Family Members*, 21 December 2010.

24 Öberg, Marko Divac, "The Legal Effects of Resolutions of the UN Security Council and General Assembly in the Jurisprudence of the ICJ," *European Journal of International Law*, Volume 16, Issue 5 (November 2005), pp. 879–906.

25 Nifosi-Sutton, Ingrid, *The Protection of Vulnerable Groups under International Human Rights Law*, Routledge: Abingdon, UK 2017, p. 76.

26 UN Human Rights Committee, *Toonen v. Australia*, Communication No. 488/1992, 31 March 1994.

27 UN Committee on the Elimination of Racial Discrimination, *Concluding Observations (India)*, 17 September 1996, para 14.

28 Piccone, Ted, "The Future of UN Special Procedures," in Scott Sheeran and Sir Nigel Rodley, Eds., *Routledge Handbook of International Human Rights Law*, Routledge: Abingdon, UK 2013, p. 726.

29 UN Office of the High Commissioner for Human Rights, "Mission Statement," accessed at www.ohchr.org/EN/AboutUs/Pages/Mission Statement.aspx on 8 May 2019.
30 UN Free and Equal, "The United Nations' Global Campaign against Homophobia and Transphobia," accessed at www.unfe.org/about/ on 8 May 2019.
31 Nifosi-Sutton, op. cit. 25, p. 4.
32 Ibid., p. 5.
33 Ibid., p. 111.

2　Categorical enlargement

As demonstrated in Table 1.2 in the prior chapter, there are 27 different characteristics, including variant phrasings or formulations of characteristics, found explicitly in the text of the nine core international human rights treaties. None of these categories, however, is explicitly defined or delimited within these texts. As discussed, the Vienna Convention on the Law of Treaties provides a rigorous framework for interpreting the meaning of treaties, yet also one that allows for flexibility and evolution in how critical words and phrases are to be understood. In a human rights context, the VCLT bodes particularly well for the strategy of *categorical enlargement*, given that the meaning of many terms and concepts in the human rights field is in a constant state of evolution.

This chapter will consider three case studies of the use of this strategy: (1) the "minority rights" framework, which has great potential for the use in protecting vulnerable groups, but thus far has undergone only limited categorical enlargement; (2) the now well-established enlargement of "descent" to cover the hundreds of millions of people who are oppressed on the basis of caste and analogous systems of inherited status; and (3) the emerging use of "colour" to cover discrimination against persons with albinism.

The "minority rights" framework and its limitations

Given the ordinary meaning of the word "minority," the issue of "minority rights" would appear to, tautologically, be the rights of those who are in some numerical smaller category within any particular social or political context. Considering the focus of human rights, it may also logically follow that minority rights would pertain primarily to groups in non-dominant positions of the sort that would render them vulnerable to human rights violations by the state and/or by dominant societal actors. Thus, taken only this far, the term "minority" would appear to have application to a wide range of vulnerable groups. However, in practice the term has been defined restrictively and has, at least thus far, largely resisted evolution in a way that would enable maximal application of the term to the protection of vulnerable populations.

Most of the earliest IHR treaties, including the ICESCR and the ICERD make no reference to minorities as such. However, Article 27 of the ICCPR does briefly specify that persons belonging to "ethnic, religious or linguistic minorities shall not be denied the right, in community with the other members of their group, to enjoy their own culture, to profess and practise their own religion, or to use their own language." This definition was largely reinforced in 1992 by the Declaration on the Rights of Persons Belonging to National or Ethnic, Religious and Linguistic Minorities. The Declaration somewhat expanded the terminology beyond "ethnic, religious, or linguistic" minorities to include "national" minorities. However, it did so without clarifying how a "national minority" is to be differentiated from other minorities, other than implying that that a national minority is one whose status relates to the territory and population of a specific nation-state.[1]

The focused use of the word "minorities" in wording of the ICCPR and in the subsequent 1992 Declaration has often been interpreted as a binding limitation, which is to say that the term "minorities" under IHR law refers only to national, ethnic (inclusive of racial), religious, and linguistic minority groups. Some interpretations of the term have suggested even narrower parameters, such as that it applies only to minorities with a geographically concentrated presence or with a long-term historical residence within the territory of a state.[2] Thus, such interpretations largely exclude immigrant communities from recognition as minorities even when they are ethnically, religiously, or linguistically distinct.[3] Similarly, other vulnerable groups whose characteristics are not linked to ethnicity, religion, or language fall completely outside the purview of minority protections: "persons not so linked, even if they form a numerical minority, and even if subject to violence, discrimination, or other violations of human rights," wrote Heinze, "are indeed entitled to human rights protections, but not to minority rights."[4]

Such rigid interpretations of the term "minority" have been subject to contestation. Arguing for a broader interpretation of minority rights, Heinze states:

> Determinations of minority status must proceed according to functional, not only formal, criteria. The minority concept otherwise runs the risk of betraying the purposes of human rights law through rigid application of definitions designed to serve other purposes, and thus of excluding groups for whom minority status is certainly no less, but also no more, artificial.[5]

He cites in particular the potential utility of the concept of "sexual minorities" to cover homosexual and bisexual persons.[6] Likewise, Packer argues that "effective responses to efforts to exclude some potential beneficiaries from protection of established standards require determinations in case-specific situations" and that these should derive "from an accurate appreciation of the genuine needs of persons finding themselves in a vulnerable position warranting special protections and possibly positive entitlements."[7]

Given the potential breadth of the framework of minority rights, it could yet come to be used to extend protections to various new categories of vulnerable groups. In fact, in recent years, as will be seen later, there has been some degree of movement in this direction. In particular, a recent past Special Rapporteur on minority issues (referred to later as the SR on Minorities), Rita Izsák, tentatively extended her writ to cover some, although not all, groups with "minority-like" characteristics (such as caste, discussed in the next section).[8] Beginning in 2017, her successor in the role, Fernand de Varennes, noted as one of his priorities for the mandate to further explore "[t]he scope and meaning of the term 'minority' as contained in the Declaration on the Rights of Minorities and article 27 of the International Covenant on Civil and Political Rights." He also introduced a substantive emphasis on inclusion of "deaf and hearing impaired persons as members of linguistic minorities."[9]

In general, however, the limits of the minority framework demonstrate the need for the strategy of categorical enlargement to be applied more vigorously to other existing protected characteristics. The next sections review two such cases, both relating to the anti-racial discrimination provisions of the ICERD. The first, originating in the 1990s and continuing down to the current day, applies the characteristic of "descent" to cover groups who experience systemic societal oppression on the basis of the hereditary status of caste. The other, initiated within the last decade, applies the category of "colour" to cover the severe human rights violations experienced by persons with the genetic condition albinism.

"Descent" and caste-based oppression

Although it is one of the most ancient and most persistent forms of societal oppression, the relegation of human beings to "untouchable" status under the Hindu caste system has only been addressed by IHR law since the mid-1990s. The Constitution of India promulgated in 1950 took steps to prohibit untouchability and to promote the advancement of so-called "scheduled castes" or "Dalits," but in practice progress has been limited and uneven. According to the International Dalit Solidarity Network (IDSN), a Copenhagen-based NGO, some 260 million Dalits are still subject to severe deprivation and ongoing human rights violations, principally in India but also in Nepal, Bangladesh, Sri Lanka, and in some South Asian diaspora communities. IDSN contends that

> caste systems divide people into unequal and hierarchical social groups. Those at the bottom are considered "lesser human beings," "impure" and "polluting" to other caste groups. They are known to be "untouchable" and subjected to so-called "untouchability practices" in both public and private spheres.

As such, Dalits are often subjected to society's most demeaning and hazardous jobs, including forced labor, and.

> [d]ue to exclusion practiced by both state and non-state actors, they have limited access to resources, services and development, keeping most Dalits in severe poverty. They are often de facto excluded from decision making and meaningful participation in public and civil life.

IDSN further argues that the

> hierarchical division of a society placing inherent privileges and restrictions by birth run contrary to the belief that 'all human beings are free and equal in dignity and rights' as stated in Article 1 of the Universal Declaration of Human Rights.[10]

As such, the group argues, "Caste discrimination involves massive violations of civil, political, economic, social and cultural rights. Caste-affected communities are denied a life in dignity and equality."[11]

Despite such manifest, longstanding, and persistent violations of the human rights of hundreds of millions of people, the international system was decidedly slow to act. In the context of IHR law, this pattern of neglect can be explain in part by the absence of the term "caste" in any of the international human rights treaties, seemingly placing the issue beyond the scope of IHR law. Other protected characteristics also did not appear to be applicable, given that Dalits are members of the same racial, ethnic, national, linguistic, and religious groups as those of other Hindu castes within their societies. As argued by Keane,

> When increasingly well-organised and vocal Dalit human rights organisations began successfully highlighting the widespread discrimination on the basis of caste still taking place in India and other areas of South Asia, and the failure of domestic policies to tackle the issue, there was a need to find a precise source of international legal obligations for the eradication of caste-based discrimination in these countries.[12]

In the 1990s, CERD began to address caste in its Concluding Observations to country reports, and in particular to India starting in 1996.[13] However, the most important breakthrough took place in 2002 by means of the strategy of categorical enlargement, when CERD issued its General Recommendation XXIX.[14] This document focuses specifically on the term "descent," which appears in ICERD Article 1(1) alongside "race," "colour," and "national or ethnic origin." Given that each of these terms appear in parallel with the term "race," it is implied that each has its own distinct substantive content.

From this point of departure, General Recommendation XXIX Preamble paragraph 7 stated, for the first time, that "discrimination based on 'descent' includes discrimination against members of communities based on forms of social stratification such as caste and analogous systems of inherited status which nullify or impair their equal enjoyment of human rights." Paragraph 1(a) then specified a range of factors that could be indicative of caste discrimination, including:

> inability or restricted ability to alter inherited status; socially enforced restrictions on marriage outside the community; private and public segregation, including in housing and education, access to public spaces, places of worship and public sources of food and water; limitation of freedom to renounce inherited occupations or degrading or hazardous work; subjection to debt bondage; subjection to dehumanizing discourses referring to pollution or untouchability; and generalized lack of respect for their human dignity and equality.

This position marked an emergence from dormancy for the use of the term "descent," whose originally intended meaning is somewhat opaque. In a review of the *travaux préparatoires* of the ICERD with regard to "descent," Keane found that the term was actually added at the suggestion of India, although for reasons that are unclear.[15] However, given that "caste" and "descent" are listed as separate terms in the Constitution of India, Keane argues that the two terms would *not* have been regarded by the Indian delegation as synonymous. In light of the evolutive nature of IHR law, Keane concludes that how this history

> affects the current interpretation of the meaning of descent is a hermeneutical question, answered by underlining the authority of [the treaty-monitoring body] CERD to dynamically interpret the terms of the Constitution, and the necessity of affording the Committee the freedom to do so.[16]

He also notes that

> Ultimately, descent is a term of convenience. It allows international human rights bodies to examine legitimate claims of continuing caste-based discrimination. CERD should not pretend

that descent originally meant caste, when it did not. It should recognize that it has re-interpreted the term.[17]

Whatever the debates about the provenance of the term "descent," what is certain is that the initiative by CERD established a much firmer basis for IHR law to pursue the protection of those oppressed on the basis of caste status. In 2000, the now-defunct UN Subcommission on the Promotion and Protection of Human Rights also passed a resolution that, without ever using the term "caste," declared that "discrimination based on work and descent is a form of discrimination prohibited by international human rights law."[18] The resolution calls for states to take "all necessary constitutional, legislative and administrative measures" and to ensure "appropriate legal penalties and sanctions" to identify, deter, and punish discrimination based on work and descent. The resolution also galvanized a consultative process through which a draft set of "Principles and Guidelines for the Effective Elimination of Discrimination Based on Work and Descent" were developed. The Principles and Guidelines enunciate the rights of "all persons of affected communities to enjoy, on an equal footing with others, all civil, political, economic, social and cultural rights" (para 2).[19] Discrimination on the basis of "work and descent" was given an expansive definition inclusive of "inherited status such as caste, including present or ancestral occupation, family, community or social origin, name, birth place, place of residence, dialect and accent" (para 2).

With caste having now been clearly established as covered under IHR law, approaches to descent-based discrimination have continued to evolve. The term "descent" now clearly extends beyond South Asian Dalits to other "analogous systems of inherited status" including the *buraku* of Japan, the Muhamasheen of Yemen, and the Haratine people of Mauritania.[20] A compilation of UN documents assembled by IDSN reveals a proliferation of UN engagement on caste-related discrimination over the period since 1996. The compilation found that, as of July 2017, seven different treaty bodies have issued a total of 86 recommendations to countries regarding caste. Likewise, the first cycle (2008–2013) of the Universal Periodic Review at the Human Rights Council included 43 caste-specific recommendations. Further, 20 different Special Procedures have addressed caste, including SPs relating to slavery, food, water, housing, health, education, poverty, torture, religion, violence against women, and freedom of expression.[21]

SR on Minorities Rita Izsák also engaged on the issue of caste, making it the focus of her 2016 annual report, which stated that "while many caste-affected groups may belong to the same larger ethnic, religious, or linguistic community, they often share minority-like characteristics, particularly their non-dominant and often marginalized position, stigma, and historic use of the minority rights framework to claim their rights" (para 21).[22] Such a position, a welcome departure from a more-rigid interpretation of "minority" rights, may in itself represent another emerging application of evolutive interpretation in general and of categorical enlargement in particular.

"Colour" and discrimination against persons with albinism

Another, still-fledgling, use of categorical enlargement can be seen in the expansion of efforts to extend human rights protections to persons with albinism. Albinism is a genetically inherited condition that causes a lack of melanin in skin, hair, and eyes and is characterized by a distinctive phenotypical expression present from the time of birth. The condition appears in all sexes, ethnicities, and countries of the world at rates ranging from 1 in 17,000–20,000 people in North America and Europe to as frequently as 1 in 1,000 in parts of sub-Saharan Africa. Lack of pigmentation causes vulnerability to sun and to bright light, usually resulting in at least some degree of visual impairment and a heightened risk for skin cancer.[23]

Person with albinism (or PWAs, a term preferred to the vernacular "albinos") are also subjected to a wide range of human rights violations. Some of these are similar to abuses experienced by other stigmatized populations, including social ostracism to severe that can inhibit PWAs' ability to obtain an education, earn a living, and receive appropriate health care. Certain other egregious human rights violations are unique to the situation of PWAs, most notably "ritual attacks" rooted in superstitious beliefs. A Canada-based NGO, Under the Same Sun, states that: "In Tanzania, people with albinism are called *zeru zeru*, meaning 'ghosts.' It is assumed by some that these 'ghosts' bleed a different colour, or even that they are immortal." Such beliefs have led to multiple attacks on PWAs:

> A baby born with albinism may be considered a curse and be killed. [I]gnorance and superstitions [fuel] beliefs that people with albinism possess magical qualities. They spread the lie that the body parts of people with albinism used in charms and potions bring wealth, power and good luck.

The group reports that since 2006, more than 520 such attacks on PWAs were recorded in 28 countries.[24]

The situation of PWAs has only quite recently begun to be noted by the major organs of the UN. In 2013, the Human Rights Council adopted a resolution expressing its concern at "attacks against persons with albinism, including against women and children, which are often committed with impunity" and "the widespread discrimination, stigma and social exclusion suffered by persons with albinism" (preamble paras 7–8).[25] Upon the recommendation of the Human Rights Council, the General Assembly proclaimed 13 June to be International Albinism Awareness Day, beginning in 2015.[26] More substantively, the Council also requested a preliminary report from OHCHR; in response, OHCHR concluded that "[o]verall, the human rights situation of persons with albinism has received little attention from Member States, the international community and human rights advocates. International and regional human right mechanisms have only sporadically raised the issue" (para 60).[27] This report was followed by a more in-depth study from the Human Rights Council Advisory Committee.[28] Collectively, these reports raised awareness of such key issues as ritual attacks and trafficking in body parts, infanticide and abandonment of babies, and social stigmatization and bullying of school children. Equally importantly, the reports began the process of discerning two distinct bases for bringing the plight of PWAs into the ambit of IHR law: "disability" and "colour."

Although albinism per se is more accurately described as a condition than a disability, lack of pigmentation in the eyes does often lead to visual impairments that clearly fall within the scope of the Convention on the Rights of Persons with Disabilities (CRPD), which in Article 1 states that "[p]ersons with disabilities include those who have long-term physical, mental, intellectual or sensory impairments which in interaction with various barriers may hinder their full and effective participation in society on an equal basis with others."[29] PWAs may also need specialized attention with regard to skin cancer prevention and treatment, ophthalmic and optical care, and associated social support in schools and places of employment. However, the visual impairments associated with the condition of albinism manifestly do not fully capture the scope and severity of the human rights abuses to which many PWAs are subjected. Indeed, other persons with comparable visual impairments caused by conditions other than albinism do not experience the same sorts of stigmatization, bullying, or ostracism endured by PWAs, much less the ritual attacks, infanticide, or human trafficking. These human rights violations thus are not rooted in PWAs' visual disabilities but much more deeply in the extreme stigmatization caused by societal reactions to their appearance in general and more specifically to their eye, hair, and skin color.

"Colour" appears as a protected characteristic in several major IHR treaties, including the earliest three: ICCPR, ICESCR, and ICERD. In these covenants it is invariably listed immediately after race and has largely been understood to be synonymous with race. Indeed, the concept of color has been, and continues to be, under-defined. One comprehensive book on racial discrimination, published in 2011, examined the ICERD and other elements of IHR law over the course of 380 pages of text. The issue of color, however, was dispatched in just three paragraphs. The author, Diaconu, concludes:

> On one side, the concepts of race and ethnic or national origin undoubtedly cover, to a large extent, that of colour. On the other hand, taking into account the mixture of populations, the nuances of skin colour are unlimited, which makes it difficult to establish categories and, consequently, to analyse the situation on such a basis. Therefore, it is not necessary to give more space to the concept of colour.[30]

Other scholars, however, have found more room for debate. In a law review article on "skin color and human rights advocacy," Aceves argues that

> While race and color are often used interchangeably, it is important to treat color as a distinct category. Race and color do not always match. This distinction is also significant in light of

growing concerns about the legitimacy of racial categories and the continuing impact of skin color on human behavior. In [the United States] and throughout the world, the difference between life and death can often be measured by degrees of pigmentation.[31]

While much of Aceves's argument relates to differential treatment experienced by people of lighter versus darker complexions, he also uses the example of discrimination against PWAs living among members of their own "race."

In recent years, the UN system has likewise moved towards a recognition of bias against PWAs as related explicitly to their "colour." In 2015, based on the recommendation of its Advisory Committee, the Human Rights Council mandated a new Independent Expert on the enjoyment of human rights by persons with albinism (referred to below as the IE on PWAs). In her initial survey of the root causes of anti-PWA attacks and discrimination, the IE on PWAs argued that "[t]he appearance of persons with albinism makes them stand out, particularly in environments where the majority of the population have darker pigmentation and the contrast between the two groups is stark."[32] She thus concluded that

> Persons with albinism are therefore a visible minority group whose appearance and colouring has made them subjects of instantaneous discrimination. Their stigma, the lifelong social exclusion and general discrimination they face, is a similar experience to that of vulnerable racial minorities because of their skin colour. This factor leaves open the possibility of addressing this root cause under laws prohibiting "racial discrimination" on the "ground" of "colour."[33]

The IE on PWAs has acknowledged the relevance of disability discrimination for PWAs, but has drawn particular attention to "discrimination based on skin tone or shade, including *within the same ethnic group*. While discrimination based on skin colour is an everyday reality for most persons with albinism, discourse on discrimination based on colour has rarely been applied to albinism" (emphasis added).[34] She also made a clear argument for evolutive interpretation by means of categorical enlargement, specifying that "there is potential to address albinism under the International Convention on the

Elimination of All Forms of Racial Discrimination, as the governing concept is not 'race' but 'racial discrimination,' which may be based on any of five 'grounds': race, colour, descent, national origin and ethnic origin."[35]

In August 2016, CERD tentatively agreed, stating in its Concluding Observations to reports from South Africa that it "expresses concern on the discrimination and stigmatization faced by persons with albinism, on the basis of colour."[36] Further evolutive interpretation from CERD, from the IE on PWAs, and from other sources seems likely to continue to clarify the relationship between racial discrimination and the persecution of PWAS specifically due to their color, including in cases in which they share the same racial or ethnic identity as their persecutors.

In all, as with the cases of "descent" and caste, the strategy of categorical enlargement is a promising one for the protection of the human rights of persons with albinism. Nonetheless, there remain many vulnerable populations that do not plausibly fit into an existing category within the texts of existing IHR treaties; instead, they are subjected to their own distinctive patterns of intersectional and compounded discrimination. In such cases, broader thinking is required, including for some vulnerable populations, the construction of novel heuristic frameworks that may have no fixed existing definition under IHR law. This strategy of "conceptual expansion" is the subject of the next chapter.

Notes

1 UN General Assembly, *Declaration on the Rights of Persons Belonging to National or Ethnic, Religious and Linguistic Minorities*, 20 December 1993.
2 Medda-Windischer, Roberta, *Old and New Minorities: Reconciling Diversity and Cohesion*, Nomos: Baden-Baden, Germany 2009, pp. 58–59.
3 Ibid., pp. 41–42.
4 Heinze, Eric, "The Construction and Contingency of the Minority Concept," in Deirdre Fottrell and Bill Bowring, Eds., *Minority and Group Rights in the New Millennium*, Martinus Nijhoff: Leiden, Netherlands 1999, p. 42.
5 Ibid, p. 74.
6 Ibid., p. 69.
7 Packer, John, "Problems in Defining Minorities," in Deirdre Fottrell and Bill Bowring, Eds., *Minority and Group Rights in the New Millennium*, Martinus Nijhoff: Leiden, Netherlands 1999, pp. 225–226.

8   UN Human Rights Council, *Report of the Special Rapporteur on Minority Issues on Minorities and Discrimination based on Caste and Analogous Systems of Inherited Status*, 28 January 2016, para 36–39.
9   UN Human Rights Council, *Report of the Special Rapporteur on Minority Issues*, 16 January 2018, para 31–33.
10 International Dalit Solidarity Network, "What Is Caste Discrimination?" accessed at http://idsn.org/caste-discrimination/what-is-caste-discrimination/ on 27 August 2017.
11 Ibid.
12 Keane, David, *Caste-based Discrimination in International Human Rights Law*, Ashgate: Farnham, UK 2007, p. 8.
13 UN Committee on the Elimination of Racial Discrimination, *Concluding Observations (India)*, 17 September 1996, para 14.
14 UN Committee on the Elimination of Racial Discrimination, *General Recommendation XXIX on Article 1, Paragraph 1, of the Convention (Descent)*, 1 November 2002.
15 Keane, op. cit. 12, p. 227 passim 232.
16 Ibid., pp. 215–216.
17 Ibid., p. 237.
18 UN Sub-Commission on the Promotion and Protection of Human Rights, *Discrimination based on Work and Descent,* 11 August 2000.
19 UN Human Rights Council, "Principles and Guidelines for the Effective Elimination of Discrimination based on Work and Descent," included in: *Final report of Mr. Yozo Yokota and Ms. Chin-Sung Chung, Special Rapporteurs on the Topic of Discrimination based on Work and Descent*, 18 May 2009.
20 UN Human Rights Council, op. cit. 8.
21 International Dalit Solidarity Network, "Caste Discrimination and Human Rights: A Comprehensive Compilation," accessed at http://idsn.org/wp-content/uploads/2017/07/UN-Compilation.pdf on 27 August 2017.
22 UN Human Rights Council, op. cit. 8.
23 UN Independent Expert on Persons with Albinism, *Report of the Independent Expert on the Enjoyment of Human Rights by Persons with Albinism*, 18 January 2016.
24 Under the Same Sun, "Superstition & Witchcraft: Dangerous Myths and Stigma Surround People with Albinism," accessed at www.underthesamesun.com/content/issue#what-is-albinism on 27 August 2017.
25 UN Human Rights Council, *Technical Cooperation for the Prevention of Attacks against Persons with Albinism*, 24 September 2013.
26 UN Human Rights Council, *Initiatives Taken to Raise Awareness and Promote the Protection of the Rights of Persons with Albinism*, 12 June 2015.
27 UN Office of the High Commissioner for Human Rights, *Report of the Office of the United Nations High Commissioner for Human Rights: Persons with Albinism*, 12 September 2013.

28 UN Human Rights Council, *The Report of the Human Rights Council Advisory Committee on the Study on the Situation of Human Rights of Persons Living with Albinism*, 10 February 2015.
29 UN General Assembly, *Convention on the Rights of Persons with Disabilities*, 13 December 2006.
30 Diaconu, Ion, *Racial Discrimination*, Eleven International Publishing: The Hague, Netherlands 2011, pp. 59–60.
31 Aceves, William J., "Two Stories about Skin Color and International Human Rights Advocacy," *Washington University Global Studies Law Review*, Volume 14 (2015), pp. 563–564.
32 UN Human Rights Council, *Report of the Independent Expert on the Enjoyment of Human Rights by Persons with Albinism*, 29 July 2016, para 68.
33 Ibid.
34 UN Human Rights Council, *Report of the Independent Expert on the Enjoyment of Human Rights by Persons with Albinism*, 18 January 2016, para 33.
35 Ibid.
36 UN Committee on the Elimination of Racial Discrimination, *Concluding Observations on the Fourth to Eighth Periodic Reports of South Africa*, 26 August 2016, para 20.

3   Conceptual expansion

As demonstrated in the prior chapter on categorical enlargement, one crucial strategy for the extension of human rights protections to new categories of vulnerable populations is to apply evolutive interpretation to the existing terms used within human rights treaties. However, this strategy has its limits and may not be plausible for all characteristics or for all vulnerable groups.

In some cases, the particular pattern of human rights violations experienced by a group may be related to more than one characteristic. When both such characteristics are already protected under IHR law, it may then be possible to apply classic "intersectional" analysis in which multiple characteristics are considered not in isolation but rather with regard to their cumulative effect upon the individual. Such intersectional analysis is commonly done, for instance, in addressing the human rights violations of women who are also members of ethnic, religious, or linguistic minorities, and thus experience multiple simultaneous and synergistic forms of discrimination.

In other cases, however, it becomes necessary to develop and deploy novel heuristic frameworks, making use of terms with no fixed existing definitions under IHR law, in order to fully ascertain and address complex patterns of compounded discrimination. This is the strategy of *conceptual expansion*, and this section will examine three ongoing examples of its use: (1) the well-established concept of "xenophobia" as applied to a broadly "anti-stranger" or "anti-foreigner" bias; (2) the emerging term "Afrophobia" with regard to members of the African diaspora who suffer on the basis of negative associations with a continent; and (3) a tentatively emerging framing of a "multifaceted Roma universe" which seeks to more accurately characterize Roma/Gypsy peoples, and the widespread biases against them, from that vulnerable population's own perspective.

"Xenophobia" and intolerance of "the stranger"

The term "xenophobia" appears prominently in the titles of a number of important human rights documents, including a resolution of the Commission on Human Rights, a declaration from a major world conference, and an ongoing Special Procedure of more than 20-years tenure. Almost invariably, "xenophobia" appears alongside two of the most extensively defined terms in IHR law, namely "race" and "racial discrimination." Yet curiously, at the time it first came into widespread use xenophobia had – and today still has – no official status as a term under IHR law. According to a 2016 report by Report of the Special Rapporteur on contemporary forms of racism, racial discrimination, xenophobia and related intolerance (referred to below as the SR on Racism): "There is no internationally recognized legal definition of xenophobia, not even in the various international and regional policy instruments that seek to combat this phenomenon."[1]

Rather, xenophobia emerged as a concept out of the need to address serious human rights violations related to people being perceived as "strangers" – outsiders, foreigners, members of "out groups." The SR on Racism adopted a definition of xenophobia as "behaviour specifically based on the perception that the other is foreign to or originates from outside the community or nation."[2] Such xenophobia manifests itself

in multiple forms that could be characterized according to the severity, scale and modality of expression. At the most severe, xenophobia could lead to the expulsion or eradication of population groups. At the other end, manifestations of xenophobia could range from bullying to mild hate speech. Between these extremes, there is a range of practices, including political scapegoating, administrative exclusion, selective and restrictive immigration policies, targeted gang violence, police harassment, profiling and stereotyping in the media.[3]

Notably, while xenophobic discrimination may often correlate with distinctions in race, ethnicity, language, or religion, such differences need not be present. Indeed, and importantly, xenophobia can also be directed against individuals by others from *within* the same racial, ethnic, linguistic, or religious groups. Introduced because it was perceived to be needed, xenophobia as a term has developed an extensive presence in the lexicon of IHR law without having ever been mentioned in any of the core treaties. As such, it represents an important example of the use of the strategy of conceptual expansion.

The idea of xenophobia itself has ancient roots, being derived from the Ancient Greek words for fear of the strange or foreign. As a term used in the UN context, however, it appeared rather abruptly in the early 1990s. As late as 1989, an ECOSOC resolution on the Second Decade to Combat Racism and Racial Discrimination made no mention of the term.[4] But by 1992, the Sub-Commission on the Prevention of Discrimination and Protection of Minorities called for appointment of "a special rapporteur to address the issue of contemporary forms of racism, racial discrimination and xenophobia."[5] This Special Procedure was created the following year, roughly at the same time that the Vienna Declaration and Programme of Action included "racism, racial discrimination, xenophobia and other forms of intolerance" as one of its major subheadings.[6]

Xenophobia as a term received its most prominent platform when it was included in the 2001 Declaration of the World Conference against Racism, Racial Discrimination, Xenophobia and Related Intolerance.[7] In the Declaration, xenophobia is almost invariable invoked as part of the overall formula rather than as a freestanding form of discrimination. Still, it is clear that the drafters of the Declaration were concerned about human rights abuses directed at those who were perceived as strangers, foreigners, or outsiders. Article 16 makes this clear:

> We recognize that xenophobia against *non-nationals, particularly migrants, refugees and asylum-seekers*, constitutes one of the main sources of contemporary racism and that human rights violations against members of such groups occur widely in the context of discriminatory, xenophobic and racist practices. (italics added)

A 2001 publication jointly produced by OHCHR and several other UN agencies on "International Migration, Racism, Discrimination, and Xenophobia" sheds greater light on the thinking behind the concept of xenophobia at that time. It states that

> while racism generally implies distinction based on difference in physical characteristics, such as skin coloration, hair type, facial features, etc., xenophobia denotes behavior specifically based on the perception that the other is foreign to or originates from outside the community or nation.[8]

The publication also notes the novelty of the inclusion of the term: "The definition of xenophobia, and its differentiation from racism and racial discrimination, are still evolving concepts."[9]

Perhaps most importantly for present purposes, the publication also strikes at the heart of why a conceptual expansion was necessary:

> In many cases, it is difficult to distinguish between racism and xenophobia as motivations for behaviour, since differences in physical characteristics are often assumed to distinguish the "other" from the common identity. However, manifestations of xenophobia occur against people of identical physical characteristics, even of shared ancestry, when such people arrive, return or migrate to States or areas where occupants consider them outsiders.[10]

The report goes on to elucidate a range of human rights violations inflicted upon migrants, including human trafficking, cross-border smuggling, labor exploitation, and targeted violence, and also outlines how xenophobic reactions by local populations and governments exacerbate the plight of many migrants.

The timing of the inclusion of the word "xenophobia" in the IHR lexicon in the early 1990s clearly seems related to major global changes that were accelerating at that time. Much of the international movement against racism had long been focused on battling *apartheid* in South Africa. But by the early 1990s, the progressive abolition of *apartheid* was well underway, and this created political space for increased attention to other facets of racism. At the same time, numerous borders were being opened up through economic processes related to globalization and political processes associated with the collapse of the Soviet Union and its sphere of influence.

Since that time, application of the concept of xenophobia has been particularly prominent in the work of the SR on Racism, the mandate for which has been continuously renewed since 1994. While the plight of migrants has largely been central to the SR on Racism's analysis of xenophobia, other angles have also been explored at length; these have included "the rise of isolationism worldwide and the increasing prevalence of xenophobic rhetoric in political discourse" (2004)[11] and how "the fight against terrorism was restricting the economic and social rights restricting the economic and social rights of communities affected by xenophobia" (2005).[12]

Although xenophobia has become well entrenched as a term used in human rights discourse since 2001, it has thus far failed to achieve a full and clear definition. However, this may be changing. In light of recurrent and expanding international crises relating to the maltreatment of refugees and migrants, the SR on Racism focused his entire 2016 annual report specifically on the meaning and content of the term "xenophobia." In this report, the SR noted forthrightly that "international law defines neither xenophobia nor xenophobic discrimination" (para 2).[13] The report, therefore, aims "to bring clarity to the concept of xenophobia, provides an overview of the different applicable norms and frameworks prohibiting xenophobia that have been adopted at the international, regional and national level, and discusses manifestations of the phenomenon of xenophobia" (para 2). One of the report's conclusions (para 68) is that

> given the ambiguity surrounding the notion of xenophobia, there is a need for a more robust research agenda that seeks to consider the sources of xenophobia and the effectiveness of the strategies in place to counter xenophobia, taking into consider intersectionality, scale, and the multitude of actors involved.

In all, a striking feature of the discussion of xenophobia has been that its underdeveloped definition has *not* led to calls to abandon its use but rather arguments for adding rigor to its intellectual and conceptual basis. The continuing, and indeed recently intensifying, use of the term "xenophobia" indicates that the strategy of conceptual expansion applied in this case has come to be regarded not only as a legitimate form of evolutive interpretation but as an essential one in the current era.

"Afrophobia" and persons of African descent

A more recent, if still closely related, use of the strategy of conceptual expansion can be found in the focus placed on people of African descent living in diaspora from the continent. As with xenophobia, this area of focus has its roots in the Declaration of the 2001 World Conference, which stated (para 33):

> We consider it essential for all countries in the region of the Americas and all other areas of the African Diaspora to recognize the existence of their population of African descent and the cultural, economic, political and scientific contributions made by that population.[14]

Drawing attention to human rights violations against this vulnerable group, the Declaration went on (para 33) to call for all countries to

> recognize the persistence of racism, racial discrimination, xenophobia and related intolerance that specifically affect them, and recognize that, in many countries, their long-standing inequality in terms of access to, inter alia, education, health care and housing has been a profound cause of the socio-economic disparities that affect them.[15]

To advance these ends, the Declaration called for the creation of a Working Group on persons of African descent (referred to below as the WG on AD), which was established in 2002 as a Special Procedure. In many ways, the WG on AD has operated largely within well-established existing parameters relating to race, ethnicity, descent, and racial or ethnic origin. However, the WG on AD has also introduced some new dynamics, since no parts of existing IHR law specifically address issues of diaspora or of descent from one particular *continent*. Partly in reaction to this lacuna, the WG on AD has begun to employ the strategy of conceptual expansion by means of an entirely new and previously undefined term: "Afrophobia."

Definitions of this concept remain fluid and under development. In the 2013 report of the WG on AD, Afrophobia was described as "an assertion of the special and unique form of discrimination faced by people of African descent" and called for "assuring its equal use with analogous terms that are used to address the stigmatization and prejudice against ethnic, religious and other vulnerable groups" (para 52).[16] The WG on AD's 2014 country report on Sweden noted "with satisfaction" that the Swedish government had begun using the term Afrophobia to describe "discrimination based on lack of knowledge of the African continent . . . [that] affected people of African origin or descent" (para 42).[17] In this context, the WG on AD provides the most comprehensive definition yet (para 43) of Afrophobia as a social force that

> seeks to dehumanize and deny the dignity of a large group of people defined by visible characteristics of difference, in this case, their skin colour, imagined psychological or behavioural traits and also by invisible ones, in particular their relation with Africa as a continent (understood as primitive).

Although the term Afrophobia has already begun to achieve currency, it remains quite a recent coinage. The term does not appear in the mandate of the WG, nor in the 2013 General Assembly resolution creating the International Decade for People of African Descent,[18] nor in the 2001 World Conference on Racism's Declaration and Programme of Action.[19] Further, the term also does not appear to have been in wide circulation for very long even in scholarly publications about the UN. A Google Scholar search using both of the terms "Afrophobia" and "United Nations" retrieves no results before 1983; 6 uses between 1983 and 2000; and 20 uses between 2001 and 2010; but 208 uses between 2011 and 2018.[20]

This last period overlaps with the introduction of the term into UN discourse in 2011. As explained by then-chair of the WG on AD, Mirelle Fanon Mendes-France, "Afrophobia was a specific concept, brought forward by civil society, which identified persons who had been victims of racism and racial discrimination because they had come from the African continent or belonged to the African diaspora." The WG on AD called upon the Human Rights Council to begin to use the term,[21] and it did so in 2012 via resolution 21/33, stating in para 13 that it "[d]eplores the special form of discrimination faced by people of African descent known as 'Afrophobia.'"[22]

Since then, the new construct of Afrophobia has entered into regular use by the WG on AD as part of its often-repeated formulation of "racism, Afrophobia, racial discrimination, xenophobia and related intolerance."[23] The 2014 WG on AD report also provided a specific human rights framing to Afrophobia, arguing that it serves to "historicize the transatlantic trade in captured Africans and enslavement, and to sequence from the other forms of racism coming after that as crimes against humanity." In the same document, a civil society participant applied the term Afrophobia to the controversial Dutch Christmas tradition of Zwarte Piet (Black Pete), which includes the use of blackface makeup (para 43).

Thus far, the concept of Afrophobia does not appear to have come into common usage within the UN system beyond the WG on AD. For example, none of the recommendations made to states during the first two cycles of the Universal Periodic Review process made use of the term.[24] Nor does "Afrophobia" appear in any of the annual reports submitted by CERD since 2011. Still, there is some evidence of its adoption in other less formal quarters. For example, a statement by the OHCHR's 2016 Fellows of People of African Descent used the term alongside other much-longer established ones at the 2016 session of the UN Forum on Minority Issues, stating that African migrants to Europe "face systematic racism, racial discrimination, xenophobia and Afrophobia."[25]

Likewise in February 2017, a written statement submitted to the Human Rights Council by the International Youth and Student Movement for the United Nations was titled "People of African Descent: Recognizing and Combating Afrophobia."[26] In this case, the term "Afrophobia" was not simply included as part of a list, but rather the statement made a substantive argument in favor of its use. In particular, the statement claims Afrophobia as a successor to the term "negrophobia," which was included in the first mandate of the SR on Racism but quickly thereafter fell out of use, due in large part to the outdatedness of the word "negro" in English. The statement argued,

> While the replacement of negrophobia with Afrophobia was discussed in that connection, it did not take place and therefore deprived people of African descent the recognition it had

previously had in listings of existing forms of discrimination. It is therefore a timely measure . . . to reintroduce this recognition of the special and unique form of discrimination that people of African descent face.

In all, Afrophobia has not yet become a universal term of usage or even settled into a definitive meaning. However, as the example of xenophobia demonstrates, new terms can become entrenched and proliferate. Afrophobia has already entered into human rights discourse despite lacking a textual basis in any human rights instruments, thereby providing further evidence of the potential for the strategy of conceptual expansion.

The "multifaceted Roma universe"

There can be little doubt about the persistence and severity of the human rights violations endured by the geographically dispersed, linguistically heterogeneous, and culturally diverse peoples known in Europe by such names as Gypsies, Travelers, Kale, Manouche, Sinti, and/or Roma. For at least 500 years, these groups (which will be referred to here as Roma/Gypsy) have resided in many different empires, regions, and countries, and alongside numerous ethnic, religious, and linguistic groups, without ever becoming fully assimilated or accepted into those societies.

Liegeois suggests a three-party typology for the centuries-long forms oppression of experienced by these peoples: "policies of exclusion," including banishment, expulsion, and mass murder; "policies of confinement," including limitations on mobility, de facto enslavement, and deportation to colonies; and "policies of assimilation" such as prohibition of Roma/Gypsy customs, language, and dress.[27] So widely acknowledged is the past and present damage wrought by these practices that Liegeois does not even feel the necessity to make the case for their continuing impact: "No detailed factual account is needed to show how difficult living conditions are for Roma, so extensive are their issues: all the national and international reports make this clear."[28]

Yet if the empirical data are all too available, there remain significant conceptual problems in identifying how best to define the population in question. In an examination of the evolution of political categories within the European Union, Simhandl identifies three distinct phases through which the construction of the category has progressed. The first was a period in the 1970s during which geographic mobility (alternatively referred to as itineracy, nomadism, caravandwelling, or simply having "no fixed abode") was the defining criterion. In the mid-1990s, after the collapse of the Communist regimes of Europe, "a second interpretive pattern developed: the term 'Roma' was increasingly used, the characterization as 'minority' gained importance, and the boundaries of the discourse were geographically re-drawn, this time around 'Eastern Europe.'"[29]

Both of these first two phases were problematic, Simhandl argues, because neither nomadism as a way of life nor "ethnicity" as a category adequately captures the full and complex realities of the Roma/ Gypsy experience. Importantly, neither approach accurately reflects how these peoples *understood themselves*. This was perhaps inevitable, Simhandl argues, because the aim of most European studies was that "knowledge was to be gathered *about* 'Gypsies' not *from* them. . . . Making the people themselves participants in the discourse by asking *them* about such issues was not even considered as an option at that time."[30] However, Simhandl is hopeful that human rights discourse may have more recently entered into a new third phase that she terms "Roma – from object to subject?"

Within the UN, the most prominent statement about the rights of the Gypsy/Roma population during this period was CERD's General Recommendation XXVII in 2000. While this document is careful to address the substantive human rights violations committed against this population, it elides questions of definition. Beyond associating anti-Gypsy bias with "racial discrimination," the document never specifies which of its five protected characteristics – race, color, descent, national or ethnic origin – applies to Roma/Gypsies. Rather, General Recommendation XXVII calls upon states to "[t]o respect the wishes of Roma as to the designation they want to be given and the group to which they want to belong" (para 3).[31]

A more proactive approach was taken more by SR on Minorities Rita Izsák, whose website prominently highlighted Roma/Gypsy issues as one of three substantive "Issues in Focus," alongside linguistic minorities and minority women and children. Concerns about the Roma/Gypsies were cited in numerous of the SR's reports, including on such topics as hate speech and incitement to hatred in the media, the prevention of violence and atrocities against minorities, the inclusion of minority issues in post-2015 development agendas, and policies leading to deprivation of citizenship. Likewise, Roma/Gypsy issues were addressed by means of the SR's country missions to France, Greece, Bulgaria, Hungary, Ukraine, and Bosnia and Herzegovina.[32]

The SR on Minorities was careful to keep her discussion of the persecution of Roma clearly within the ambit of IHR law. She adopted the Council of Europe's definition of "anti-Gypsyism" as "a specific form of racism, an ideology founded on racial superiority, a form of dehumanization and institutional racism nurtured by historical discrimination, which his expressed, among others, by violence, hate speech, exploitation, stigmatization, and the most blatant type of discrimination."[33] The SR notes that "[a]nti-Gypsyism therefore includes strong anti-Roma prejudices and stereotypes, including those that lead to labelling Roma communities as criminal, aggressive, or as 'parasites' on welfare systems."[34]

At the same time, however, the SR sought to shift the frame of reference beyond traditional notions of race and ethnicity and towards a more tailored understanding of the unique experience of the Roma/Gypsies. She did so by introducing some novel heuristics: "The term Roma thus does not denote a specific group, but rather refers to the multifaceted Roma universe" and "is therefore a multidimensional term that corresponds to the multiple and fluid nature of Roma identity." In a field such as IHR law that replies upon legal definitions and clearcut categories, this is a notable use of the strategy of conceptual expansion.

Compared to the introduction and proliferation of the terms "xenophobia" and "Afrophobia," this use of conceptual expansion is a subtle and still nascent one. However, it could mark a significant step towards the goal identified by Simhandl of recognizing the Roma/Gypsies as subjects rather than merely objects within the discourse of IHR law.

This broader lens has already produced some results by helping to shift discussion way from primarily conceptualizing the Roma/Gypsies merely as one ethnic minority among many in Eastern Europe. For example, the SR convened a workshop in Brasilia in 2015 to focus on the long-neglected populations of Roma who reside in the Americas as a result of processes of European colonization. These overlooked populations are among the most discriminated against, socially and economically marginalized, and politically subordinated members of the societies in which they live [but] largely invisible. . . . This invisibility contributes to a vicious circle of marginalization and exclusion, and leads to neglect by the authorities and policymakers.[35]

In some ways, this substantive focus on diaspora issues connects with and reinforces the other patterns of conceptual expansion discussed in this book on cross-cultural migrants and persons of African descent.

Of course, it remains to be seen whether efforts to expand framings of a "multifaceted Roma universe" will result in further and more inclusive coverage of all Roma/Gypsy peoples within IHR law. Nonetheless, the use on conceptual expansion in this case marks a significant effort to allow Roma peoples to exercise greater self-determination in how their communities, cultures, and individual lives are framed and understood.

In all, the use of the strategy of conceptual expansion offers promise, but also runs risks. Unlike the strategy of categorical enlargement, conceptual expansion moves discussions of IHR law well beyond the texts of treaties. While the case of some vulnerable groups may demand such innovative thinking, some other case can be approached not by stretching the boundaries of IHR law but rather by returning to its foundational principles: that all individuals deserve to have their human rights defended vigorously and effectively. Sometimes, as discussed in the next chapter, this may entail, taking conscious and proactive steps to identify the group-level characteristics that can jeopardize individuals who share certain statuses, identities, or conditions.

Notes

1 UN Human Rights Council, *Report of the Special Rapporteur on Contemporary Forms of Racism, Racial Discrimination, Xenophobia and Related Intolerance*, 13 May 2016, para 26.
2 Ibid.
3 UN Human Rights Council, *Report of the Special Rapporteur on Contemporary Forms of Racism, Racial Discrimination, Xenophobia and Related Intolerance*, 9 May 2017, para 11.

4 UN Economic and Social Council, *Resolution on Implementation of the Programme of Action for the Second Decade to Combat Racism and Racial Discrimination*, Resolution 1989/6, 23 February 1989.

5 UN Commission on Human Rights, *Report of the Secretary-General: Implementation of the Programme of Action for the Second Decade to Combat Racism and Racial Discrimination*, 2 December 1992.

6 UN General Assembly, *Vienna Declaration and Programme of Action*, 12 July 1993.

7 UN World Conference against Racism, Racial Discrimination, Xenophobia and Related Intolerance, *Declaration*, 8 September 2001.

8 International Labour Office (ILO), International Organization for Migration (IOM), Office of the United Nations High Commissioner for Human Rights (OHCHR) In consultation with the Office of the United Nations High Commissioner for Refugees (UNHCR), "International Migration, Racism, Discrimination, and Xenophobia," August 2001, p. 10, accessed at http://publications.iom.int/system/files/pdf/interna tional_migration_racism.pdf on 27 August 2017.

9 Ibid.

10 Ibid.

11 UN Human Rights Council, op. cit. 1, para 9.

12 Ibid.

13 UN Human Rights Council, op. cit. 1.

14 UN World Conference, op. cit. 7.

15 Ibid.

16 UN Human Rights Council, *Report of the Working Group of Experts on People of African Descent on Its Twelfth Session*, 22-April 26 April 2013.

17 UN Human Rights Council, *Report of the Working Group of Experts on People of African Descent on Its Sixteenth Session, Addendum Mission to Sweden*, 25 August 2015.

18 UN General Assembly, *Proclamation of the International Decade for People of African Descent*, 23 December 2013.

19 UN World Conference, op. cit. 7.

20 Google Scholar search conducted by the author on 19 May 2019.

21 UN Human Rights Council, *Report of the Working Group of Experts on People of African Descent on Its Tenth Session*, 28 March–1 April 2011.

22 UN Human Rights Council, *Report of the Human Rights Council on Its Twenty-First Session*, 11 November 2015.

23 UN Human Rights Council, *Report of the Working Group of Experts on People of African Descent on Its Seventeenth and Eighteenth Sessions*, 19 July 2016.

24 Search conducted by the author of the database of UPR Info, accessed at www.upr-info.org/database/ on 25 July 2017.

25 UN Office of the High Commissioner for Human Rights, *Ninth Session of the Forum on Minority Issues on Minorities in Situations of Humanitarian Crises, Statement by the 2016 Fellows of People of African Descent*, 24–25 November 2016.

26 UN Human Rights Council, *People of African Descent: Recognizing and Combating Afrophobia: Written Statement by the International Youth and Student Movement for the United Nations, a Nongovernmental Organization in General Consultative Status*, 13 February 2017.
27 Liegeois, Jean-Pierre, *The Council of Europe and Roma: 40 Years of Action*. Council of Europe Publishing: Strasbourg, France 2012, pp. 27–28.
28 Ibid., p. 28.
29 Simhandl, Katrin, "Beyond Boundaries? Comparing the Construction of the Political Categories 'Gypsies' and 'Roma' Before and After EU Enlargement," in Nando Sigona and Nidhi Trehan, Eds., *Romani Politics in Contemporary Europe: Poverty, Ethnic Mobilization, and the Neoliberal Order*, Palgrave Macmillan: London, UK 2009, p. 75.
30 Ibid.
31 UN Committee on the Elimination of Racial Discrimination, *General recommendation XXVII on discrimination against Roma*, 16 August 2000.
32 UN Office of the High Commissioner for Human Rights, *Human Rights of Roma in the Special Rapporteur's Thematic Reports (to the Human Rights Council and the UN General Assembly)*, accessed at www.ohchr.org/EN/Issues/Minorities/SRMinorities/Pages/ReportsRoma.aspx on 27 August 2017.
33 UN Human Rights Council, *Report of the Special Rapporteur on Minority Issues, Rita Izsák: Comprehensive Study of the Human Rights Situation of Roma Worldwide, with a Particular Focus on the Phenomenon of Anti-Gypsyism*, 11 May 2015, para 12.
34 Ibid.
35 UN Human Rights Council, *Regional Workshop on the Situation of Roma in the Americas*, 10 March 2016, para 14.

4   Group-conscious universal application

As has been seen in the preceding sections, the evolutive interpretation of human rights treaties can sometimes make use of the categorical enlargement of existing human rights protections, while at other times conceptual expansion can be employed to frame broader patterns of human rights violations so that they can be more effectively addressed. However, when such strategies are not optimal, or even viable, for a particular population, much can still be achieved through the third strategy of *group-conscious universal application*.

This strategy represents a proactive reassertion of the starting point of all IHR law, namely its application to all individual human beings. It contends that fully understanding and combating some patterns of human rights violations requires the use of a group-specific lens – even if that group's shared characteristic is not explicitly found within the texts of IHR instruments. This strategy follows two main approaches: first, that universal rights can effectively be defended by identifying distinct social groups as falling under broad "other status" provisions or, second, by asserting that the effective universal defense of individuals requires recognition of group-level characteristics that contribute to their vulnerability.

The first mode of application for this strategy represents a return to the texts of the core human rights treaties. Most of the IHR treaties include open-ended provisions for "other status." The Human Rights Committee, perhaps because it has the longest and most extensive record of interpreting a specific treaty, has applied this category most frequently. It has done so quite judiciously, however, electing not to use "other status" to declare entirely new categories of protected characteristics but rather primarily as an element in its evaluation of individual complaints. Over time, the Human Rights Committee has discerned individual cases of discrimination under "other status" on a number of grounds, including the place of residence within a state, public or private nature of schooling, being employed or unemployed, the composition of households, age, or characteristic such as marital status, health status, and "dwarfism."[1] "Other status" provisions have also been applied by other treaty bodies, including CESCR (e.g., for sexual orientation, social status, and refugee or migrant status)[2] and CRC (e.g., for pregnancy and number of children).[3] Nonetheless, in a comprehensive, book-length study of the views of treaty bodies on equality and non-discrimination between 1976 and 2005, Vandenhole concluded that "[i]t is striking to see how few complaints pertaining to discrimination on the basis of 'other status' have been found to be well-founded. The widening of the phrase 'other status' clearly has not been matched by an equally-expanding number of instances of prohibited discrimination."[4]

Thus "other status" provisions may have a role to play, but they are not a panacea for the extension of protections to new categories of vulnerable populations. An important complementary approach involves the recognition that many treaty provisions provide listings that manifestly are *not* intended to be exhaustive, as signaled by the commonly used phrasing "distinctions of any kind, *such as . . .*" (emphasis added). This phrasing points back to the fundamentally universal nature of human rights, in that they apply to *all* people in *all* places.

The next section will examine three cases of group-conscious universal application: (1) persons affected by leprosy, as a distinct group suffering from an ancient stigma in the modern world; (2) older persons, as a group defined by an often vulnerable position within the human life course; and (3) LGBT people, as a group who possess a sexual orientation and/or gender identity which render them vulnerable to multiple forms of oppression.

Persons affected by leprosy: human rights confronting an ancient stigma

Although Hansen's disease, more commonly known as leprosy, is today a readily treatable bacterial infection, the longstanding fear and stigmatization of people with the severely disfiguring disease lingers to the modern day. So too do the legacies of extreme social and legal measures taken for compulsory quarantining of people with leprosy under terrible conditions in so-called "leper colonies." As described by the Human Rights Council in 2016,

> In the ancient era, leprosy was perceived by different societies, religious beliefs, and cultural practices as highly contagious, hereditary, and received as a divine punishment. Moreover, the lack of scientific knowledge of the causative organism of the disease, as well as its mode of transmission and lack of effective remedy, which can lead to various degrees of physical disfigurement, have also contributed to the stigma and discrimination against persons affected by leprosy and their family members.[5]

It may seem counterintuitive that the issue of leprosy should have emerged onto the agenda of the human rights community in the modern era, but lingering associations of the disease with "uncleanness," sinfulness, contamination, and contagion have been perpetuated down to the current day. For example, Japan did not repeal the last of its coercive quarantining and forced hospitalization laws until 1996, nor did the United States until 1997.[6] This is the case despite modern scientific knowledge that the disease is not in fact highly transmissible, has been treatable since the 1940s, and has been entirely curable since the 1980s; indeed, an estimated 16 million people have been cured of the disease and global prevalence has dropped from more than 5 million at highest estimates to less than 200,000 by 2015.[7]

A 2010 effort by the Human Rights Council Advisory Committee afforded new prominence to the issue through the creation of draft "Principles and Guidelines to address discrimination against persons with leprosy and their family members."[8] The 13 Guidelines cover such topics as equality and non-discrimination, home and family life, employment, housing, education, and health care. The Advisory Committee noted that some manifestations of leprosy do clearly result in disabilities, but it did not attempt the strategy of categorical enlargement. Nor did it propose a conceptual expansion, such as by introducing a novel conceptual framework such as "leprophobia" or "anti-leperism."

However, the Principles and Guidelines clearly do apply the third strategy of group-conscious universal application. Indeed, this document openly recognizes that bias against persons affected by leprosy and their family members cannot be adequately addressed without using a group-level lens. In fact, the Advisory Committee explicitly framed the broader relationship of the issue to the achievement of universal human rights: "The global commitment to human rights cannot be achieved if the rights of any particular group of people, such as persons affected by leprosy and their family members, are not fully respected or protected."[9]

The Principles and Guidelines make repeated efforts to reckon with the reality that the social ostracism, isolation, and marginalization of persons affected by leprosy is rooted less in any actual risk of contagion than in irrational reactions to a disfigured physical appearance and in superstition concerning a stigmatized group identity. Examples of the use of group-level universal application can be found in Guideline 1 prohibiting policies that "forcefully or compulsorily segregate and isolate persons on the grounds of leprosy" in a discriminatory manner and without appropriate medical grounds; Guideline 4 supporting "the reunification of families separated in the past as a result of policies and practices"; Guideline 5 ensuring that affected persons "are not obliged to accept a particular living arrangement because of their disease"; and Guideline 9 calling for removal of "discriminatory language, including the derogatory use of the term 'leper' or its equivalent in any language or dialect."[10]

In a number of ways, the issues raised with regard to leprosy bear resemblances to the approach taken to albinism, as discussed in Chapter 2. So too did the next step of the UN institutional response, namely the mandating in 2017 of a Special Rapporteur on the topic (referred to here as the SR on Leprosy).[11]

In her first report the SR on Leprosy documented "thousands of years of human rights abuses and violations" (section III.A), noting that the disease "came to embody what was socially prescribed as shameful and disrupting, and was thus rendered something beyond it mere disease. It became a symbol, a powerful metaphor." (para 25).[12] Moving to a discussion of the current era, the SR on Leprosy emphasizes the issue of "vulnerability" in its manifestations both at the individual and group levels. On the one hand, any individual may potentially become infected by *Mycobacterium leprae* and suffer its damaging effects on the human body. However, members of some groups who are already characterized by vulnerability (such as due to poverty or migrant status) are less likely to have access to public health preventative measures and early diagnosis and are more likely to be deprived of timely and appropriate treatment. Once infected, member of such groups are frequently subjected to compounded discrimination based on their original sources of vulnerability alongside their new status as stigmatized "lepers." Such discrimination is often extended to members of their families who may or may not themselves have leprosy but can be perceived nonetheless as "contaminated."

It can thus be seen that in order to achieve universal application of human rights norms with regard to *individuals with the disease of leprosy*, it is necessary to use a group-conscious lens with regard to the human rights violations faced by *people with social condition of leprosy*. The symmetry here is clear and the issue is seemingly uncontroversial; the vote for the SR on Leprosy's mandate was enacted by the Human Rights Council without need for a vote.[13] More complex, however, are the next two examples in this chapter of vulnerable populations: older people, whose numbers are increasing greatly worldwide, and LGBT people, for whom stigmatization and discrimination is far from a historical relic or a marginal experience.

Older people: human rights across the lifespan

According to OHCHR,

> Population ageing constitutes one of the most significant demographic transformations of the 21st century. For the first time in history, humankind will reach a point at which there are fewer children than older persons in the world. Approximately 700 million people, or 10 per cent of the world's population, are over the age of 60. It is estimated that by 2050, the number of older persons will have doubled reaching 20 per cent of the global population.[14]

This growing population of older persons, according to the Human Rights Council, faces

> a number of particular challenges in the enjoyment of their human rights that need to be addressed urgently, including in the

areas of prevention of and protection against violence and abuse, social protection, food and housing, right to work, equality and non-discrimination, access to justice, education, training, health support, long-term and palliative care, lifelong learning, participation and accessibility.[15]

Despite the growing size and clear vulnerability of many members of the older population, IHR law has yet to develop a clear, coherent, or consistent response. A 2013 report submitted to the Human Rights Council concluded that

> while most international human rights instruments are applicable to all age groups, including older persons, a number of human rights issues that are particularly relevant to older persons have not been given sufficient attention either in the wording of existing human rights instruments or in the practice of human rights bodies and mechanisms.[16]

Indeed, as noted in Table 1.1, only the ICMW and CRPD include age as a fully protected characteristic. Other references are more limited. CEDAW Article 11(e) mentions that women in "old age" must have equal access to social security programs,[17] and CRPD Article 16(2) calls for programs and services for disabled people to be "age-sensitive."[18] This, however, essentially exhausts explicit reference to old age within the core IHR treaties. (The foundational Universal Declaration of Human Rights, although not directly legally binding, also refers in Article 25(1) to "the right to security in the event of . . . old age."[19])

A significant number of soft law instruments have also addressed ageing, prominently including the United Nations Principles for Older Persons (1991)[20] and the Political Declaration and the Madrid International Plan of Action on Ageing (2002).[21] However, the future prospects for a binding international covenant remain unclear. Some advocates have called for such a treaty, arguing by analogy to the Convention on the Rights of the Child, but others find reason for caution in this comparison.

> The emergence of the idea of the CRC is the recognition of children, as a class, as having rights in addition to those of adults. . . .

Older people are adults and have rights to autonomy – the challenge for the international and national communities is to ensure that those rights are respected the same way as other adults.[22]

A new treaty singling out older people, it may be argued, could "promote an image of older age as necessarily dependent and vulnerable" and can "risk infantilising older people" and thus depriving them of personal agency.[23]

In the absence of such a treaty, or even of consensus about how to frame the issue of older people, a range of actors within the UN system have taken steps to extend protections. For example, in 2010, the General Assembly created an Open-ended Working Group on Ageing;[24] in 2011, the Secretary General submitted a report on ageing to the General Assembly;[25] and in 2014 the Human Rights Council created a mandate for an Independent Expert on the enjoyment of all human rights by older persons (referred to here as the IE on Older Persons), which was added without dissent and therefore without need for a vote.[26] Two of the treaty bodies have also addressed this population at length: CESCR through its General Comment 6 on the economic, social, and cultural rights of older persons[27] and CEDAW by means of its General Recommendation No. 27 on older women.[28]

The strategy of conceptual expansion might have seemed to be a logical one for older people, given that the concept of "ageism" is already one in common circulation in rights discourse, albeit one without a formal status in IHR law. However, there has been little systematic or sustained effort to introduce ageism as a discrete and independent construct in IHR law. For example, the Secretary General's 2011 report includes a single paragraph that mentions "ageism" parenthetically, equates it to "prejudice against and stigmatization of older persons" and states that it is a widespread practice – but then never uses the term again.[29] In the first five annual reports produced by the IE on Ageing[30] the term is only used a total of only seven times, mostly in passing and not in ways that seek to expand upon the concept. "Ageism" appears five times in the reports produced by the UNGA Working Group, but always in the context of the term's use by civil society speakers.[31] The term is never used at all in CESCR General Comment and CEDAW General Recommendation No. 27, which are perhaps the most authoritative documents to date explicating the relationship between older people and IHR law.

In contrast, the strategy of group-conscious universal application has proven more fruitful. Indeed, this approach is explicitly articulated in the Secretary General's report, which states (para 24):

> At the international level, while "age" is not explicitly listed as a prohibited ground of discrimination in most human rights treaties, the lists are illustrative and non-exhaustive, and usually include an open-ended category ("other status") under which treaty bodies consider age-related discrimination.

and that (para 21)

> There are numerous obligations vis-à-vis older persons implicit in most core human rights treaties despite the lack of specific provisions focusing on them. Such instruments apply to older persons in the same way as to all other people, providing protection for essential human rights.[32]

The report then goes on to note the applicability also of Article 26 of the ICCPR and that the Human Rights Committee has enunciated the view that "a distinction related to age which is not based on reasonable and objective criteria may amount to discrimination on the ground of 'other status'" (para 27). Importantly, the report also explicitly frames older persons not only as individual right-holders but also as a vulnerable group: "what older persons share, as a group, is the experience of living within societies in which stereotyping, the attribution of lesser value, political disempowerment and economic and social disadvantage often accompany ageing" (para 41).

Continuing global growth in the numbers of older people, both in absolute terms and as a proportion of the population, will make ageing an increasingly salient human rights concern for the foreseeable future. On the positive side, however, is that older people are also a vulnerable group for whom dignity, autonomy, and quality of life are, at least in principle, nearly universally supported in states and societies around the world. The next case study, however, is far more controversial and contested.

LGBT people: human rights protecting sexual and gender diversity

The category of sexual orientation made its first major appearance in IHR law in the context of the 1994 ruling by the Human Rights Committee in the individual communication *Toonen v. Australia*,[33] which involved an anti-sodomy law in the Australian state of Tasmania. The Committee offered a straightforward use of the strategy of categorical enlargement, but employed only a terse statement that it "confines itself to noting . . . [that] in its view the reference to 'sex' in articles 2, paragraph 1, and 26 is to be taken as including sexual orientation" (para 8.7). The ruling does not explain the Committee's reasoning but, on its face, the linkage would appear to be that sexual orientation intrinsically involves the sex of one's romantic and sexual partners.

A great deal has transpired since 1994 with regard to legal understandings of human sexuality, and sexual orientation has become far more recognized worldwide as a freestanding concept in its own right rather than as a dimension of "sex." Numerous legal statutes around the world now directly prohibit discrimination on the basis of sexual orientation with no reference to the category of sex; particularly significant examples include the post-*apartheid* Constitution of South Africa[34] and the Treaty of Amsterdam enacted by the European Union.[35]

But while sexual orientation may now have a much clearer status conceptually and legally, the term itself still does not appear in any of the international treaties and prospects seem dim that it will in the foreseeable future. Nonetheless, more recent efforts to extend human rights protections to lesbian, gay, and bisexual people under international law have advanced through application of the strategy of group-conscious universal application to issues of sexual orientation. Likewise, the characteristics of gender identity and expression (i.e., transgender status) and sex characteristics (i.e., intersex status), although somewhat newer within IHR discourse, have increasingly come to be treated on a parallel basis. (Collectively, these five related populations are commonly rendered by the initials LGBTI; some elements of transgender identity as well as intersex issues are also considered as emerging issues in the Conclusion.

A prominent proactive assertion of SOGI-related rights is the "Free and Equal" campaign begun in 2013 by OHCHR, which describes it as "an unprecedented global UN public information campaign aimed at promoting equal rights and fair treatment of LGBTI people" and whose website, videos, factsheets, and other products are said to have reached two billion people.[36] The campaign frames the issue with a sense of urgency, stating that "[m]ore than a third of the world's countries criminalize consensual, loving same-sex relationships, entrenching prejudice and putting millions of people at risk of blackmail, arrest and imprisonment."[37] Lack of legal protections, alongside public hostility, leads to widespread discrimination, "including workers being fired from jobs, students bullied and expelled from schools, and patients denied essential healthcare."[38]

The strategy of group-conscious universal application is evident even in the name of the Free and Equal campaign itself, which derives from the opening words of Article 1 of the UDHR stating that: "All human beings are born free and equal in dignity and rights." Perhaps because the issues have already been framed so explicitly in terms of universal rights, the descriptions of the campaign itself make no effort to employ categorical enlargement (such as arguing for the relevance of "sex" as a category), nor does it attempt any conceptual expansion (beyond employing commonly used terms such as "homophobia" and "transphobia" to characterize an aversion or antipathy to these groups).

Treaty bodies have followed a similar trajectory of using group-conscious universal application. For example, in its 2016 General Comment on the implementation of the rights of the child during adolescence, the CRC condemns so-called "conversion therapies" intended to change a child's sexual orientation, urges repeal of discriminatory laws, and exhorts states to protect LGBTI children from "all forms of violence, discrimination or bullying by raising public awareness and implementing safety and support measures" (para 34).[39] Although only one paragraph makes direct reference to sexual orientation in this General Comment, it is notable that the CRC makes no particular effort to specify a legal basis for its statement. Implicit in its reasoning, however, is the view that the treaty's mandate to protect *all* children from violence and discrimination cannot be fulfilled without paying attention to issues of concern for this particular group of children.

CESCR's 2016 General Comment 22 on the right to sexual and reproductive health goes even further. It calls not only for an end to discrimination, violence, and harassment but also for LGBTI people "to be fully respected for their sexual orientation, gender identity and intersex status."[40] In a single paragraph (para 23), General Comment 22 distills a range of key concerns about SOGI rights:

> Criminalization of sex between consenting adults of the same gender or the expression of one's gender identity is a clear violation of human rights. Likewise, regulations requiring that lesbian, gay, bisexual transgender and intersex persons be treated as mental or psychiatric patients, or requiring that they be "cured" by so-called "treatment," are a clear violation of their right to sexual and reproductive health.

The paragraph concludes with the clear assertion that that "state parties also have an obligation to combat homophobia and transphobia, which lead to discrimination, including violation of the right to sexual and reproductive health." To date, this statement by CESCR is one of the strongest efforts ever under IHR law to apply group-conscious universal application to LGBTI people.

A similar approach has been undertaken within the two SOGI-related reports produced by OHCHR in response to Human Rights Council resolutions in 2011 and 2014. The first report used an explicitly universalist framing, stating (para 5):

> The application of international human rights law is guided by the principles of universality and non-discrimination enshrined in article 1 of the Universal Declaration of Human Rights, which states that "all human beings are born free and equal in dignity and rights." All people, including lesbian, gay, bisexual and transgender (LGBT) persons, are entitled to enjoy the protections provided for by international human rights law.[41]

It also forthrightly asserted that "[t]he obligations of States to prevent violence and discrimination based on sexual orientation and gender identity are derived from various international human rights instruments" (para 8). The report acknowledged the lack of an explicit textual basis for inclusion of sexual orientation and gender identity but then quickly explained why this did not constitute a definitive obstacle (para 7):

> The specific grounds of discrimination referred to in the International Covenant on Civil and Political Rights and other human rights treaties are not exhaustive. The drafters intentionally left the grounds of discrimination open by using the phrase "other status." Sexual orientation and gender identity, like disability, age and health status, are not explicitly mentioned among the grounds listed.

Three years later, the 2014 OHCHR report on SOGI issues continued the use of group-conscious universal application but also went a step further in contenting thats (para 10),

> states have well-established obligations to respect, protect and fulfil the human rights of all persons within their jurisdiction, including LGBT and intersex persons. These obligations extend to refraining from interference in the enjoyment of rights, preventing abuses by third parties and proactively tackling barriers to the enjoyment of human rights, including, in the present context, discriminatory attitudes and practices.[42]

This report laid the foundation for the next major development in this field, the creation in 2016 of a new Special Procedure, an Independent Expert on protection against violence and discrimination based on sexual orientation and gender identity (referred to here as the IE on SOGI). This was, however, a highly contested step. Indeed, even the title of this mandate itself illuminates the challenge facing this highly contested area of human rights. Whereas Special Procedures mandates on persons with leprosy and older people specify identify the group, the name of the highly stigmatized group involved here – lesbian, gay, bisexual, and transgender (LGBT) people – is nowhere to be found; the mandate instead refers only to "sexual orientation and gender identity" (SOGI). And while the mandates on older people and people with leprosy refer broadly to the "enjoyment of human rights," this one is narrowly restricted to "protection against violence and discrimination."

The language of the mandate itself is also strikingly tentative, suggesting some of the difficulties of applying group-conscious universal application to a group that is so heavily stigmatized. Rather than employing the sweeping language so often used in human rights discourse, the mandate contains numerous and unusual qualifications stressing: "the significance of national and regional particularities and various historical, cultural and religious backgrounds" (Preamble para 2); "the fundamental importance of respecting relevant domestic debates at the national level on matters associated with historical, cultural, social and religious sensitivities" (Preamble para 8); opposition to "seeking to impose concepts or notions pertaining to social matters, including private individual conduct, that fall outside the internationally agreed human rights legal framework" (Preamble para 9); and "ensuring respect for the sovereign right of each country as well as its national laws, development priorities, the various religious and ethical values and cultural backgrounds of its people" (Preamble para 10).[43]

Despite such caveats and conciliatory language, the creation this mandate was heavily contested. It was initially approved by a narrow vote of 23–18 with 6 abstentions; by comparison, recall that the mandates regarding persons with leprosy and older people were enacted without the need for a vote. Then, in a rare maneuver, a bloc of African states attempted to block its implementation at a November 2016 meeting of the UN General Assembly Third Committee by challenging its basis in international law. At that time, the ambassador from Botswana stated his country's opposition to focusing on people "on the grounds of their sexual interests and behaviours, while ignoring that intolerance and discrimination regrettably exist in various parts of the world, be it on the basis of colour, race, sex or religion, to mention only a few." He added that African countries contended that sexual orientation and gender identity "are not and should not be linked to existing international human rights instruments."[44]

Perhaps in response to such a high level of contention, the initial report by the first IE on SOGI, Vitit Muntarbhorn, was built around the overarching theme of "Diversity in Humanity, Humanity in Diversity" and took the route of group-conscious universal application (para 2):

> Everyone has some form of sexual orientation and of gender identity. . . . Even though human rights are inherent to everyone and involve protection for all persons without exception, regrettably persons with an actual or perceived sexual orientation and/ or gender identity diverging from a particular societal concept

are at times targeted for violence and discrimination, and violations are pervasive in numerous settings.[45]

The second IE on SOGI, Victor Madrigal-Borloz, has extended the use of group-conscious universal application, re-asserting in his first report that "[t]he mandate is anchored in universally accepted human rights principles" (para 3) and condemning common state policies that apply a sort of reverse universalism or "negation" by adopting "the position that violence and discrimination based on sexual orientation or gender identity to not exist in a particular context or that, in a given social context, there are no [LGBT] persons" (para 62).[46] His second report signaled an increasing turn towards a focus specifically on gender identity and expression, extensively documenting why pathologization of some forms of gender violates universal rights, stating that (para 20),

> the right to effective recognition of one's gender identity is linked to the right to equal recognition before the law established in article 6 of the Universal Declaration of Human Rights, subsequently set out in international human rights law, beginning with article 16 of the International Covenant on Civil and Political Rights, and also present in other universal human rights treaties and regional human rights instruments.[47]

Cumulatively, the approaches taken in recent years by the OHCHR and the IE on SOGI solidify the basis for inclusion of LGBT people within the ambit of IHR law. However, these developments also reveal the need to continue to balance a focus on universal individual rights with the use of a group-level lens. Given that, in many cases, bias against LGBT people can derive as much from their perceived affiliation with a stigmatized identity group as from their own individual sexual orientation and/or gender identity. Thus it will be essential to continue to emphasize both halves of the formulation of "group-conscious" and "universal application."

Notes

1 Vandenhole, Wouter, *Non-Discrimination and Equality in the View of the UN Human Rights Treaty Bodies*, Intersentia: Cambridge, UK 2005, p. 128 passim 133.
2 Ibid., p. 140 passim 145.

3 Ibid., p. 173 passim 179.
4 Ibid., pp. 131–132.
5 UN Human Rights Council, *Progress Report on the Implementation of the Principles and Guidelines for the Elimination of Discrimination against Persons Affected by Leprosy and Their Family Members*, 29 July 2016, para 14.
6 Ibid., para 16.
7 Ibid., para 19.
8 UN Human Rights Council, *Draft Set of Principles and Guidelines for the Elimination of Discrimination against Persons Affected by Leprosy and Their Family Members*, 12 August 2010.
9 UN Human Rights Council, op. cit. 5, para 25.
10 UN Human Rights Council, op. cit. 8.
11 UN Human Rights Council, *Elimination of Discrimination against Persons Affected by Leprosy and Their Family Members*, 22 June 2017.
12 UN Human Rights Council, *Report of the Special Rapporteur on the Elimination of Discrimination against Persons Affected by Leprosy and Their Family Members*, 25 May 2018.
13 UN Human Rights Council, op. cit. 11.
14 UN Office of the High Commissioner for Human Rights, "The Independent Expert on the Enjoyment of All Human Rights by Older Persons," accessed at www.ohchr.org/EN/Issues/OlderPersons/IE/Pages/IEOlderPersons.aspx on 27 August 2017.
15 UN Human Rights Council, *Resolution 33/5: The Human Rights of Older Persons*, 5 October 2016, para 1.
16 UN Human Rights Council, *Summary Report of the Consultation on the Promotion and Protection of the Human Rights of Older Persons*, 1 July 2013.
17 UN General Assembly, *International Convention on the Elimination of All Forms of Racial Discrimination*, 21 December 1965.
18 UN General Assembly, *Convention on the Rights of Persons with Disabilities*, 13 December 2006.
19 UN General Assembly, *Universal Declaration of Human Rights*, 10 December 1948.
20 United Nations General Assembly, *United Nations Principles for Older Persons*, 16 December 1991.
21 Second World Assembly on Ageing, *Madrid International Plan of Action on Ageing*, 8–12 April 2002.
22 Williams, John, "An International Convention on the Rights of Older People?" in Marco Odello and Sofia Cavandoli, Eds., *Emerging Areas of Human Rights in the 21st Century: The Role of the Universal Declaration of Human Rights,* Routledge: Abingdon, UK p. 141.
23 Ibid.
24 UN Division for Social Policy and Development, "Open-Ended Working Group on Ageing for the Purpose of Strengthening the Protection of

the Human Rights of Older Persons," accessed at https://social.un.org/ageing-working-group/ on 27 August 2017.

25 UN Secretary-General, *Follow-Up to the Second World Assembly on Ageing Report of the Secretary-General*, 22 July 2011.

26 UN Human Rights Council, op. cit. 15.

27 UN Committee on Economic, Social, and Cultural Rights, *General Comment No. 6: The Economic, Social and Cultural Rights of Older Persons*, 7 October 1995.

28 UN Committee on the Elimination of Discrimination against Women, *General Recommendation No. 27 on Older Women and Protection of Their Human Rights*, 16 December 2010.

29 UN Secretary-General, op. cit. 25.

30 UN Office of the High Commissioner for Human Rights, "Independent Expert on Ageing: Annual Reports," accessed at www.ohchr.org/EN/Issues/OlderPersons/IE/Pages/Reports.aspx on 19 May 2019.

31 UN Division for Social Policy and Development, op. cit. 24.

32 UN Secretary-General, op. cit. 25.

33 UN Human Rights Committee, *Toonen v. Australia*, Communication No. 488/1992, 31 March 1994.

34 Constitutional Assembly of South Africa, *Constitution of the Republic of South Africa*, 10 December 1996.

35 Council of the European Union, *Treaty of Amsterdam Amending the Treaty on European Union, the Treaties Establishing the European Communities and Related Acts*, 10 November 1997.

36 UN Office of the High Commissioner for Human Rights, "About UN Free and Equal," accessed at www.unfe.org/about/ on 27 August 2017.

37 Ibid.

38 Ibid.

39 UN Committee on the Rights of the Child, *General Comment No. 20 on the Implementation of the Rights of the Child during Adolescence*, 6 December 2016.

40 UN Committee on Economic, Social and Cultural Rights, *General Comment No. 22 on the Right to Sexual and Reproductive Health*, 2 May 2016.

41 UN Office of the High Commissioner for Human Rights, *Discriminatory Laws and Practices and Acts of Violence against Individuals Based on Their Sexual Orientation and Gender Identity*, 17 November 2011.

42 UN Office of the High Commissioner for Human Rights, *Discrimination and Violence against Individuals based on Their Sexual Orientation and Gender Identity*, 4 May 2015.

43 UN Human Rights Council, *Protection against Violence and Discrimination based on Sexual Orientation and Gender Identity*, 15 July 2016.

44 "African States Fail to Block United Nations' LGBT Rights Protector," *The Guardian*, 21 November 2016, accessed at www.theguardian.com/world/2016/nov/21/african-states-fail-block-united-nations-lgbt-rights-protector on 9 May 2019.

45 UN Human Rights Council, *Report of the Independent Expert on Protection against Violence and Discrimination based on Sexual Orientation and Gender Identity*, 19 April 2017.

46 UN Human Rights Council, *Report of the Independent Expert on Protection against Violence and Discrimination based on Sexual Orientation and Gender Identity*, 11 May 2018.

47 UN Human Rights Council, *Report of the Independent Expert on Protection against Violence and Discrimination based on Sexual Orientation and Gender Identity*, 12 July 2018.

Conclusion

International human rights is often precariously balanced between narrow positivist interpretations of legal texts and more expansive normative concerns about the dignity, well-being, and overall flourishing of human beings. From the former perspective, the ambit of international human rights with regard to vulnerable groups can be viewed as strictly limited to the 27 protected characteristics enumerated in the texts of the core IHR treaties. From the latter perspective, however, this list of characteristics is a floor rather than a ceiling for the extension of protections to vulnerable populations.

Fortunately, the principle of the evolutive interpretation of human rights treaties has become well-established as a means by which the "purpose and intent" of treaties can be applied to new populations and ever-changing circumstances. In the absence of a single authoritative worldwide court to adjudicate the meaning of IHR treaties, much of the work of evolutive interpretation has fallen to processes within the UN, including: declarations and resolutions enacted by the General Assembly, the Human Rights Council, and other political bodies; authoritative interpretations and decisions made by treaty-monitoring bodies; the work of UN Special Procedures; and programs carried out by UN offices and agencies, most notably OHCHR.

This book has inductively developed a new typology of three principal strategies that have been, and continue to be, employed within these UN processes in order to extend protections to new categories of vulnerable populations. Some additional new emerging populations have already been identified by civil society actors and in some countries, national-level protections have already been enacted. The potential continuing utility of the three strategies for IHR law is briefly illustrated with three examples: persons with non-binary gender identity; those susceptible to discrimination on the basis of their genetic information; and intersex individuals.

Categorical enlargement is a potentially powerful strategy but clearly has parameters delineated by the "good faith" meaning of treaties. Taken beyond the point of reasonable extrapolation from the intended meaning of terms, this strategy could undermine the integrity of treaties themselves. It is thus fortunate that, in practice, the strategy of categorical enlargement has been used quite judiciously.

One emerging area in which categorical enlargement may be of use is that of persons with "non-binary" gender identity and expression. Transgender individuals were once widely assumed to be seeking a more-or-less complete shift from "male to female" or from "female to male," assisted by various medical interventions and social adaptations. Yet this is an erroneous perception, and the actual lived experience of many transgender individuals has been closer to movement along a spectrum of gender expressions and identities rather than from a shift from out of one binary category of sex and into another.[1] As increasing numbers of individuals have come to characterize their gender identity and expression as "non-binary," the category of "sex" has been reconceptualized in ways that sometimes allow for a third, non-binary option, such as for use in government-issued identity documents. This has occurred both in notably progressive countries, such as Canada, and also in more conservative countries where the idea of a "third sex" has cultural resonance, such as India.[2]

The addition of a third option with regard to the category of "sex" within IHR law would represent a clearcut and potentially useful application of the strategy of categorical enlargement. At the same time, this approach runs the risk of reifying a new single stable "third sex" category out of what is in fact a heterogeneous and fluid set of experiences and identities. Thus, categorical enlargement might offer only a stopgap measure, with broadening notions of gender identity and expression eventually also calling for complementary use of other strategies.

The strategy of *conceptual expansion* offers a more unfettered approach than categorical enlargement, since it does not rely on the literal texts of treaties. Its principal value lies in the creation of new heuristic frameworks that can aid in better defining and addressing the nature and scope of certain complex forms of compounded and intersectional discrimination. Conceptual expansion thus has a role to play with regard to vulnerable populations by providing new lenses through which they can be viewed from more innovative perspectives.

An intriguing area in which conceptual expansion might be applied is to discrimination on the basis of genetic information. Technological advances in the ability to quickly and inexpensively sequence the genome of individual humans, alongside technologies that allow of the manipulation of genes, renders this an area in which growing numbers of people are becoming susceptible to discrimination, coercion, or other unequal treatment.[3] Protection of privacy and prohibition of discrimination based on genetic information is already a category protected in numerous political jurisdictions, such as by the US federal government through the Genetic Information Nondiscrimination Act of 2008.[4] And as long ago as 1997, UNESCO sponsored a Universal Declaration on the Human Genome and Human Rights.[5]

Still, at the level of IHR law, protections remain nascent. Categorical enlargement clearly has a role to play when genetic information about a potential illness aligns with the category of "disability." There may also be room for categorical enlargement within the protected characteristic of "descent." However, given the rapid pace of advances and the emergence of unprecedented ethical quandaries relating to genetic sequencing and manipulation, categorical enlargement seems unlikely to be sufficient even in the near term. Some not-yet-coalesced form of conceptual expansion will likely be needed eventually with regard to persons subject to discrimination, or other differential treatment, based upon their genetic information.

The strategy of *group-conscious universal application* is, in some ways, the most canonical of the approaches, given that the entire system of IHR law is based upon the presumption of universality. Ideally, this strategy can move debate away from an overly atomized view of purely individual rights and towards a greater recognition of the significance of membership in certain vulnerable groups. However, it must take care to balance both group- and individual-level dimensions, and not overly weight one part or the other.

As noted, group-conscious universal application has been successfully applied to the characteristics of LGBT people and their sexual orientation and gender identity (SOGI, or sometimes SOGIE to include also gender expression). Because of its connection to biological sex and gender, the more emerging issue of intersex status has also at times addressed within the same framework, rendering the acronyms LGBTI and SOGIESC (to include "sex characteristics").

Intersex status is by no means new, and has been recognized since antiquity through the use of now-outdated terms such as "hermaphroditism" to refer to external genitalia or other physical characteristics that are neither prototypically male nor female. More modern advances have also identified various chromosomal and hormonal dimensions of intersex status. In recent times, the greater recognition of gender as a spectrum rather than a binary has further undermined rationale for early and supposedly "corrective" surgeries on intersex infants with ambiguous genitalia or for hormonal interventions at the time of puberty.[6]

Categorical enlargement with regard to "sex" or "disability" could well have utility for protecting the rights of intersex persons, as could conceptual expansion. However, the most potent approach used thus far has been the strikingly universal one of drawing explicit parallels between the widely reviled cultural practice of female genital mutilation (FGM) and the idea of "intersex genital mutilation" or IGM.[7] Activists have enunciated a compelling case that many such surgical procedures may be medically sanctioned but are not medically necessary and can result in lifelong physical and psychological suffering. One innovative approach has been to bypass the various non-discrimination provision of IHR law and instead to appeal to the Committee against Torture treaty-monitoring body to argue for the right to bodily integrity and protection to be proactively applied to infants and other people with intersex bodies.[8]

In summary, *Extending International Human Rights Protections to Vulnerable Populations* has addressed the reality that numerous vulnerable populations experience severe and systematic violations of their human rights based on the characteristics that either are not directly covered, or not fully addressed, in the existing texts of international human rights treaties. This book has inductively developed a new typology to identify and evaluate three principal strategies that are being used to extend human rights protections to new categories of vulnerable populations. The three strategies of categorical enlargement, conceptual expansion, and group-conscious universal application each differ from one another in some ways, and overlap in others. They are also by no means mutually exclusive, and can be combined with other the other strategies or with other newer approaches that, it is to be hoped, will organically arise in the future.

Notes

1 Webb, A., E. Matsuno, S. Budge, M. Krishnan and K. Balsam, "Non-Binary Gender Identities," American Psychological Association Division 44, accessed at www.apadivisions.org/division-44/resources/advocacy/non-binary-facts.pdf on 9 May 2019.
2 Open Society Foundations, "License to Be Yourself: Laws and Advocacy for Legal Gender Recognition of Trans People," May 2014, accessed at www.opensocietyfoundations.org/publications/license-be-yourself# publications_download on 9 May 2019.
3 Motoc, Iulia Voina, "The International Law of Genetic Discrimination: The Power of 'Never Again'," in Thérèse Murphy, Ed., *New Technologies and Human Rights,* Oxford University Press: Oxford, UK 2009.
4 US Equal Employment Opportunity Commission, "Facts about the Genetic Information Nondiscrimination Act," accessed at www.eeoc. gov/laws/types/genetic.cfm on 9 May 2019.
5 UN Educational, Scientific and Cultural Organisation (UNESCO), *Universal Declaration on the Human Genome and Human Rights*, 11 November 1997.
6 UN Free and Equal, "Factsheet: Intersex," accessed at www.ohchr.org/ Documents/Issues/Discrimination/LGBT/FactSheets/UNFE_FactSheet_ Intersex_EN.pdf on 9 May 2019.
7 OII Intersex Network, "Intersex Genital Mutilation," accessed at https:// oiiinternational.com/2574/intersex-genital-mutilation-igm-fourteen-days-intersex/ on 9 May 2019.
8 Stop Intersex Genital Mutilation, "UN Committee against Torture (CAT) to Investigate Intersex Genital Mutilations," accessed at http://stop.geni talmutilation.org/post/UN-Committee-against-Torture-CAT-to-investigate-Intersex-Genital-Mutilations on 9 May 2019.

Bibliography

Books and Articles

Aceves, William J., "Two Stories about Skin Color and International Human Rights Advocacy," *Washington University Global Studies Law Review*, Volume 14 (2015), pp. 563–584.

"African States Fail to Block United Nations' LGBT Rights Protector," *The Guardian*, 21 November 2016, accessed at www.theguardian.com/world/2016/nov/21/african-states-fail-block-united-nations-lgbt-rights-protector on 9 May 2019.

Belton, Brian, *Gypsy and Traveller Ethnicity: The Social Generation of an Ethnic Phenomenon*, Routledge: Abindgon, UK 2005.

Bjorge, Eirik, *The Evolutionary Interpretation of Treaties*, Oxford University Press: London, UK 2014.

Constitutional Assembly of South Africa, *Constitution of the Republic of South Africa*, 10 December 1996.

Council of the European Union, *Treaty of Amsterdam Amending the Treaty on European Union, The Treaties Establishing the European Communities and Related Acts*, 10 November 1997.

D'Amico, Francine, "LGBT and (Dis)United Nations," in Manuela Lavinas Picq and Markus Thiel, Eds., *Sexualities in World Politics: How LGBTQ Claims Shape International Relations*, Routledge: Abingdon, UK 2015, pp. 54–74.

Diaconu, Ion, *Racial Discrimination*, Eleven International Publishing: The Hague, Netherlands 2011, pp. 59–60.

Fitzmaurice, Malgosia, "The Practical Working of the Law of Treaties," in Malcolm Evans, Ed., *International Law*, 4th Edition, Oxford University Press: Oxford, UK 2010, pp. 166–200.

Focus on the Global South, "From Dream to Reality: UN Declaration on Rights of Peasants and Other People Working in Rural Areas," accessed at https://focusweb.org/from-dream-to-reality-un-declaration-on-rights-of-peasants-and-other-people-working-in-rural-areas/ on 8 May 2019.

Harris, David and Sandesh Sivakumaran, *Cases and Materials on International Law*, 8th Edition, Sweet & Maxwell: London, UK 2015.

Heinze, Eric, "The Construction and Contingency of the Minority Concept," in Deirdre Fottrell and Bill Bowring, Eds., *Minority and Group Rights in the New Millenium*, Martinus Nijhoff: Leiden, Netherlands 1999, pp. 25–86.

Keane, David, *Caste-Based Discrimination in International Human Rights Law*, Ashgate: Farnham, UK 2007.

International Dalit Solidarity Network, "Caste Discrimination and Human Rights: A Comprehensive Compilation," accessed at http://idsn.org/wp-content/uploads/2017/07/UN-Compilation.pdf on 27 August 2017.

International Dalit Solidarity Network, "What Is Caste Discrimination?" accessed at http://idsn.org/caste-discrimination/what-is-caste-discrimination/ on 27 August 2017.

International Labour Office (ILO), International Organization for Migration (IOM), Office of the United Nations High Commissioner for Human Rights (OHCHR) in Consultation with the Office of the United Nations High Commissioner for Refugees (UNHCR), "International Migration, Racism, Discrimination, and Xenophobia," August 2001, p. 10, accessed at http://publications.iom.int/system/files/pdf/international_migration_racism.pdf on 27 August 2017.

Kymlicka, Will, *Multicultural Citizenship: A Liberal Theory of Minority Rights*, Clarendon: Oxford, UK 1995.

Lerner, Natan, *Group Rights and Discrimination in International Law*, 2nd Edition, Martinus Nijhhoff: Leiden, Netherlands 2003.

Liegeois, Jean-Pierre, *The Council of Europe and Roma: 40 Years of Action*, Council of Europe Publishing: Strasbourg, France 2012.

Medda-Windischer, Roberta, *Old and New Minorities: Reconciling Diversity and Cohesion*, Nomos: Baden-Baden, Germany 2009.

Meijknecht, Anna, *Towards International Personality: The Position of Minorities and Indigenous Peoples in International Law*, Intersentia: Cambridge, UK 2001.

Moeckli, Daniel, "Equality and Non-Discrimination," in Daniel Moeckli, Sangeeta Shah and Sandesh Sivakumaran, Eds., *International Human Rights Law*, 2nd Edition, Oxford University Press: Oxford, UK 2013, pp. 157–173.

Motoc, Iulia Voina, "The International Law of Genetic Discrimination: The Power of 'Never Again'," in Thérèse Murphy, Ed., *New Technologies and Human Rights*, Oxford University Press: Oxford, UK 2009.

Nifosi-Sutton, Ingrid, *The Protection of Vulnerable Groups under International Human Rights Law*, Routledge: Abingdon, UK 2017.

Öberg, Marko Divac, "The Legal Effects of Resolutions of the UN Security Council and General Assembly in the Jurisprudence of the ICJ," *European Journal of International Law*, Volume 16, Issue 5 (November 2005), pp. 879–906.

OII Intersex Network, "Intersex Genital Mutilation," accessed at https://oii-international.com/2574/intersex-genital-mutilation-igm-fourteen-days-intersex/ on 9 May 2019.

Open Society Foundations, "License to Be Yourself: Laws and Advocacy for Legal Gender Recognition of Trans People," May 2014, accessed at www.opensocietyfoundations.org/publications/license-be-yourself#publications_download on 9 May 2019.

Packer, John, "Problems in Defining Minorities," in Deirdre Fottrell and Bill Bowring, Eds., *Minority and Group Rights in the New Millenium*, Martinus Nijhoff: Leiden, Netherlands 1999, pp. 223–274.

Pentassuglia, Gaetano, *Minorities in International Law: An Introductory Study*, Council of Europe Publishing: Strasbourg, France 2002.

Second World Assembly on Ageing, *Madrid International Plan of Action on Ageing*, 8–12 April 2002.

Sheeran, Scott and Sir Nigel Rodley, Eds., *Routledge Handbook of International Human Rights Law*, Routledge: Abingdon, UK 2013.

Simhandl, Katrin, "Beyond Boundaries? Comparing the Construction of the Political Categories 'Gypsies' and 'Roma' Before and After EU Enlargement," in Nando Sigona and Nidhi Trehan, Eds., *Romani Politics in Contemporary Europe: Poverty, Ethnic Mobilization, and the Neoliberal Order*, Palgrave Macmillan: London, UK 2009, pp. 72–93.

Stop Intersex Genital Mutilation, "UN Committee against Torture (CAT) to Investigate Intersex Genital Mutilations," accessed at http://stop.genitalmutilation.org/post/UN-Committee-against-Torture-CAT-to-investigate-Intersex-Genital-Mutilations on 9 May 2019.

UN Educational, Scientific and Cultural Organisation, *Universal Declaration on the Human Genome and Human Rights*, 11 November 1997.

Under the Same Sun, "Superstition & Witchcraft: Dangerous Myths and Stigma Surround People with Albinism," accessed at www.underthesamesun.com/content/issue#what-is-albinism on 27 August 2017.

US Equal Employment Opportunity Commission, "Facts about the Genetic Information Nondiscrimination Act," accessed at www.eeoc.gov/laws/types/genetic.cfm on 9 May 2019.

Vandenhole, Wouter, *Non-Discrimination and Equality in the View of the UN Human Rights Treaty Bodies*, Intersentia: Cambridge, UK 2005.

Webb, A., E. Matsuno, S. Budge, M. Krishnan and K. Balsam, "Non-Binary Gender Identities," American Psychological Association Division 44, accessed at www.apadivisions.org/division-44/resources/advocacy/non-binary-facts.pdf on 9 May 2019.

Williams, John, "An International Convention on the Rights of Older People?" in Marco Odello and Sofia Cavandoli, Eds., *Emerging Areas of Human Rights in the 21st Century: The Role of the Universal Declaration of Human Rights*, Routledge: Abingdon, UK pp. 128–148.

United Nations Primary Documents

International Court of Justice, *Dispute Regarding Navigational and Related Rights (Costa Rica v. Nicaragua)*, Judgment, 13 July 2009.

International Court of Justice, *Legal Consequences of the Construction of a Wall in the Occupied Palestinian Territory*, Advisory Opinion, 9 July 2004.

UN Commission on Human Rights, *Report of the Secretary-General: Implementation of the Programme of Action for the Second Decade to Combat Racism and Racial Discrimination*, 2 December 1992.

UN Committee on Economic, Social, and Cultural Rights, *General Comment No. 6: The Economic, Social and Cultural Rights of Older Persons*, 7 October 1995.

UN Committee on Economic, Social and Cultural Rights, *General Comment No. 22 on the Right to Sexual and Reproductive Health*, 2 May 2016.

UN Committee on the Elimination of Racial Discrimination, *Concluding Observations: India*, 17 September 1996.

UN Committee on the Elimination of Racial Discrimination, *Concluding Observations on the Fourth to Eighth Periodic Reports of South Africa*, 26 August 2016.

UN Committee on the Elimination of Racial Discrimination, *General Recommendation XXVII on Discrimination against Roma*, 16 August 2000.

UN Committee on the Elimination of Racial Discrimination, *General Recommendation XXIX on Article 1, Paragraph 1, of the Convention (Descent)*, 1 November 2002.

UN Committee on the Elimination of Racial Discrimination, *Stephen Hagan v. Australia*, Communication No. 26/2002, 20 March 2003.

UN Committee on the Elimination of Discrimination against Women, *General Recommendation No. 27 on Older Women and Protection of Their Human Rights*, 16 December 2010.

UN Committee on the Rights of the Child, *General comment No. 20 (2016) on the Implementation of the Rights of the Child During Adolescence*, 6 December 2016.

UN Division for Social Policy and Development, *Open-Ended Working Group on Ageing for the Purpose of Strengthening the Protection of the Human Rights of Older Persons*, accessed at https://social.un.org/ageing-working-group/ on 27 August 2017.

UN Economic and Social Council, *Resolution on Implementation of the Programme of Action for the Second Decade to Combat Racism and Racial Discrimination*, Resolution 1989/6, 23 February 1989.

UN Educational, Scientific and Cultural Organisation (UNESCO), *Universal Declaration on the Human Genome and Human Rights*, 11 November 1997.

UN Free and Equal, "Factsheet: Intersex," accessed at www.ohchr.org/Documents/Issues/Discrimination/LGBT/FactSheets/UNFE_FactSheet_Intersex_EN.pdf on 9 May 2019.

UN Free and Equal, "The United Nations' Global Campaign Against Homophobia and Transphobia," accessed at www.unfe.org/about/ on 8 May 2019.

UN General Assembly, *Convention against Torture and Other Cruel, Inhuman or Degrading Treatment or Punishment*, 10 December 1984.

UN General Assembly, *Convention on the Elimination of All Forms of Discrimination against Women*, 18 December 1979.

UN General Assembly, *Convention on the Rights of the Child*, 20 November 1989.

UN General Assembly, *Declaration on the Elimination of Discrimination against Women*, 7 November 1967.

UN General Assembly, *Declaration on the Elimination of Violence against Women*, 20 December 1993.

UN General Assembly, *Declaration on the Rights of Indigenous Peoples*, 7 September 2007.

UN General Assembly, *International Covenant on Civil and Political Rights*, 16 December 1966.

UN General Assembly, *International Covenant on Economic, Social and Cultural Rights*, 16 December 1966.

UN General Assembly, *International Convention on the Elimination of All Forms of Racial Discrimination*, 21 December 1965.

UN General Assembly, *International Convention for the Protection of All Persons from Enforced Disappearance*, 20 December 2006.

UN General Assembly, *International Convention on the Protection of the Rights of All Migrant Workers and Members of Their Families*, 18 December 1990.

UN General Assembly, *International Convention on the Rights of Persons with Disabilities*, 13 December 2006.

UN General Assembly, *Proclamation of the International Decade for People of African Descent*, 23 December 2013.

UN General Assembly, *Second Optional Protocol to the International Covenant on Civil and Political Rights, Aiming at the Abolition of the Death Penalty*, 15 December 1989.

UN General Assembly, *United Nations Principles for Older Persons*, 16 December 1991.

UN General Assembly, *Universal Declaration of Human Rights*, 10 December 1948.

UN General Assembly, *Vienna Convention on the Law of Treaties between States and International Organizations or between International Organizations*, 12 March 1986.

UN General Assembly, *Vienna Declaration and Programme of Action*, 12 July 1993.

UN Human Right Council, *Report of the Special Rapporteur on Minority Issues*, 6 January 2018.

UN Human Rights Committee, *Roger Judge v. Canada*, Communication No. 829/1998, 13 August 2003.

UN Human Rights Committee, *S. W. M. Broeks v. The Netherlands*, Communication No. 172/1984, 9 June 1987.

UN Human Rights Committee, *Toonen v. Australia*, Communication No. 488/1992, 31 March 1994.

UN Human Rights Council, *Draft Set of Principles and Guidelines for the Elimination of Discrimination against Persons Affected by Leprosy and Their Family Members*, 12 August 2010.

UN Human Rights Council, *The Human Rights of Older Persons*, Resolution 33/5, 5 October 2016.

UN Human Rights Council, *Initiatives Taken to Raise Awareness and Promote the Protection of the Rights of Persons with Albinism*, 12 June 2015.

UN Human Rights Council, *People of African Descent: Recognizing and Combating Afrophobia: Written Statement by the International Youth and Student Movement for the United Nations, a Nongovernmental Organization in General Consultative Status*, 13 February 2017.

UN Human Rights Council, "Principles and Guidelines for the Effective Elimination of Discrimination Based on Work and Descent," included in: *Final Report of Mr. Yozo Yokota and Ms. Chin-Sung Chung, Special Rapporteurs on the Topic of Discrimination based on Work and Descent*, 18 May 2009.

UN Human Rights Council, *Progress Report on the Implementation of the Principles and Guidelines for the Elimination of Discrimination against Persons Affected by Leprosy and Their Family Members*, 29 July 2016.

UN Human Rights Council, *Regional Workshop on the Situation of Roma in the Americas*, 10 March 2016.

UN Human Rights Council, *The Report of the Human Rights Council Advisory Committee on the Study on the Situation of Human Rights of Persons Living with Albinism*, 10 February 2015.

UN Human Rights Council, *Report of the Human Rights Council on Its Twenty-First Session*, 11 November 2015.

UN Human Rights Council, *Report of the Independent Expert on the Enjoyment of Human Rights by Persons with Albinism*, 18 January 2016.

UN Human Rights Council, *Report of the Independent Expert on the Enjoyment of Human Rights by Persons with Albinism*, 29 July 2016.

UN Human Rights Council, *Report of the Independent Expert on Protection against Violence and Discrimination based on Sexual Orientation and Gender Identity*, 11 May 2018.

UN Human Rights Council, *Report of the Independent Expert on Protection against Violence and Discrimination based on Sexual Orientation and Gender Identity*, 12 July 2018.

UN Human Rights Council, *Report of the Independent Expert on Protection against Violence and Discrimination based on Sexual Orientation and Gender Identity*, 19 April 2017.

UN Human Rights Council, *Report of the Special Rapporteur on Contemporary Forms of Racism, Racial Discrimination, Xenophobia and Related Intolerance*, 13 May 2016.

UN Human Rights Council, *Report of the Special Rapporteur on Contemporary Forms of Racism, Racial Discrimination, Xenophobia and Related Intolerance*, 11 August 2016.

UN Human Rights Council, *Report of the Special Rapporteur on Contemporary Forms of Racism, Racial Discrimination, Xenophobia and Related Intolerance*, 9 May 2017.

UN Human Rights Council, *Report of the Special Rapporteur on Minority Issues*, 28 January 2016.

UN Human Rights Council, *Report of the Special Rapporteur on Minority Issues on Minorities and Discrimination based on Caste and Analogous Systems of Inherited Status*, 28 January 2016.

UN Human Rights Council, *Report of the Special Rapporteur on Minority Issues, Rita Izsák: Comprehensive Study of the Human Rights Situation of Roma Worldwide, with a Particular Focus on the Phenomenon of Anti-Gypsyism*, 11 May 2015.

UN Human Rights Council, *Report of the Working Group of Experts on People of African Descent*, 5 August 2016.

UN Human Rights Council, *Report of the Working Group of Experts on People of African Descent on Its Sixteenth Session Addendum Mission to Sweden*, 25 August 2015.

UN Human Rights Council, *Report of the Working Group of Experts on People of African Descent on Its Tenth Session*, 28 March–1 April 2011.

UN Human Rights Council, *Report of the Working Group of Experts on People of African Descent on Its Twelfth Session*, 22–26 April 2013.

UN Human Rights Council, *Report of the Working Group of Experts on People of African Descent on Its Seventeenth and Eighteenth Sessions*, 19 July 2016.

UN Human Rights Council, *Summary Report of the Consultation on the Promotion and Protection of the Human Rights of Older Persons*, 1 July 2013.

UN Human Rights Council, *Technical Cooperation for the Prevention of Attacks against Persons with Albinism*, 24 September 2013.

UN Office of the High Commissioner for Human Rights, *Discriminatory Laws and Practices and Acts of Violence against Individuals based on Their Sexual Orientation and Gender Identity*, 17 November 2011.

UN Office of the High Commissioner for Human Rights, *Discriminatory Laws and Practices and Acts of Violence against Individuals based on Their Sexual Orientation and Gender Identity*, 4 May 2015.

UN Office of the High Commissioner for Human Rights, "About UN Free and Equal," accessed at www.unfe.org/about/ on 27 August 2017.

UN Office of the High Commissioner for Human Rights, "Human Rights of Roma in the Special Rapporteur's Thematic Reports (to the Human Rights Council and the UN General Assembly)," accessed at www.ohchr.org/EN/Issues/Minorities/SRMinorities/Pages/ReportsRoma.aspx on 27 August 2017.

UN Office of the High Commissioner for Human Rights, "The Independent Expert on the Enjoyment of All Human Rights by Older Persons," accessed at www.ohchr.org/EN/Issues/OlderPersons/IE/Pages/IEOlder Persons.aspx on 27 August 2017.

UN Office of the High Commissioner for Human Rights, "Mission Statement," accessed at www.ohchr.org/EN/AboutUs/Pages/MissionState ment.aspx on 8 May 2019.

UN Office of the High Commissioner for Human Rights, *Ninth Session of the Forum on Minority Issues on Minorities in Situations of Humanitarian Crises, Statement by the 2016 Fellows of People of African Descent*, 24–25 November 2016.

UN Office of the High Commissioner for Human Rights, *Report of the Office of the United Nations High Commissioner for Human Rights: Persons with Albinism*, 12 September 2013.

UN Secretary-General, *Follow-Up to the Second World Assembly on Ageing, Report of the Secretary-General*, 22 July 2011.

UN Sub-Commission on the Promotion and Protection of Human Rights, *Discrimination based on Work and Descent*, Resolution 2000/4, 11 August 2000.

UN World Conference against Racism, Racial Discrimination, Xenophobia and Related Intolerance, *Declaration*, 8 September 2001.

Index

Note: Page numbers in **bold** indicate a table on the corresponding page.

For Product Safety Concerns and Information please contact our EU
representative GPSR@taylorandfrancis.com
Taylor & Francis Verlag GmbH, Kaufingerstraße 24, 80331 München, Germany